Visit simplycm.com for more!

- Free encouraging articles and podcasts every week.
- A complete Charlotte Mason curriculum plan.
- Free e-books and video workshops.
- Simple to use Charlotte Mason homeschool resources to help you spread a rich feast of education.

America: Our Stories

Volume 1
First Peoples to 1812

By Lorene M. Lambert

America: Our Stories, Volume 1: First Peoples to 1812
© 2023 by Lorene Lambert

ISBN 978-1-61634-626-3 printed
ISBN 978-1-61634-627-0 electronic download

Published and printed by
Simply Charlotte Mason, LLC
9930 New Hope Road #11-892
Lawrenceville, Georgia 30045
simplycharlottemason.com

Printed by PrintLogic, Inc.
Monroe, Georgia, USA

Where applicable, historical quotes have been updated to reflect modern spelling, capitalization, and punctuation.

Contents

1   An American Day
    The Geography of the United States *5*

2   Until 1491
    The Native Americans *13*

3   Toscanelli's Map
    Sail West to Reach the East *23*

4   Searching for Cipango
    The Voyage of Christopher Columbus *29*

5   The Fourth Part of the World
    John Cabot and Amerigo Vespucci *37*

6   Bold Spaniards
    Conquistadors and Explorers *45*

7   The Last Voyage of the *Discovery*
    Henry Hudson *51*

8   The Lost Colony
    Roanoke *57*

9   Work to Eat
    The Adventurers of Jamestown *65*

10 Across the Vast and Furious Ocean
    The Mayflower *73*

11 New Amsterdam, New France, and New England
    The Old World Claims the New World *79*

12 The Gifts of Charles II
    More English Colonies in America *85*

13 Noble Experiments
    Pennsylvania and Georgia *91*

14 The Charter Oak
    The Seeds of Independence in the Colonies *97*

15 "Black Sam" Bellamy
    Pirates and the Triangle Trade *105*

16   "We Shall Know Better"
The French and Indian War *111*

17   Farewell, Acadia
Exiles in Louisiana and a Meeting in Albany *117*

18   Poor Richard
The Brilliant Life of Benjamin Franklin *123*

19   A Tea Party in Boston
The Causes of Revolution *131*

20   On Lexington Green
The Shot Heard 'Round the World. *137*

21   The Spirit of 1776
The Declaration of Independence *145*

22   Through the Valley of the Shadow
The War for Independence *153*

23   We the People
The Constitution of the United States *161*

24   Walking the Wilderness Road
Daniel Boone *171*

25   The Way Forward
The First Presidents *177*

26   Way Out West
The Lewis and Clark Expedition. *183*

27   Over the Pathless Oceans
The Navigations of Nathaniel Bowditch *191*

28   "Don't Give Up The Ship"
The War of 1812 . . . . *199*

29   By the Dawn's Early Light
America's Day *205*

Glossary. *213*

Endnotes *220*

Selected Bibliography. *236*

Image Sources *240*

Chapter 1

An American Day

The Geography of the United States

It's 6 A.M. on a fresh fall day in October in the United States of America.

Darkness rests like a soft quilt over the crumples and folds of the countryside. The ocean waves are crashing against the cliffs in Washington State, while early morning starlight frosts the soaring peaks of the Rocky Mountains. In the center of the country, the Mississippi River rolls ever onward, and the wind rustles the grasses of the Dakotas and ripples the leaves of mangrove trees in the Florida Everglades. On the eastern edge of the continent, along the wide Atlantic beaches, the land sleeps—and waits for day.

From the surface of the sun, 93 million miles away, the waves of light that will make a new American day speed forward, 186,000 miles every second. The light skims over the Atlantic Ocean, polishing it to a brilliant silver sheen. The earth rotates gently, a thousand miles every hour, and the light races toward the dark coastline, where the state of Maine reaches out into the cold, North Atlantic water. And there, up ahead, silhouetted against the pearly gray sky, a rounded, smooth-topped mountain surveys the rocky shore. With a satisfied glimmer, the daylight skips forward and kisses the mountain's bald head.

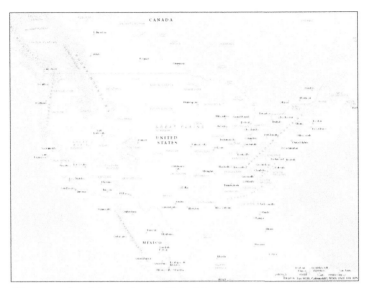

The geography of the contiguous United States

It is 6:38 A.M.; a new American day has begun. This is Cadillac Mountain, named for a French explorer. During the autumn and winter months, the sunrise touches the United States first in Maine, on Cadillac Mountain's summit. But, of course, the light doesn't stop there to rest. The day hastens on its way, shouldering the darkness aside, as America comes to life and her people begin to go about their day.

From that easternmost part of Maine, the morning light floods across the rest of the USA's east coast. It reveals a flat plain, bordered by the Atlantic Ocean, with many bays and islands, inlets and sandspits, and beautiful buff-colored beaches fringed with dunes and seagrass. This hospitable coast plays host to some of America's mightiest cities: Boston, New York City, Philadelphia. The plain stretches the whole length of the eastern shores, from Maine down to Florida. There, just a little less than an hour after it touched Cadillac Mountain, the sunrise smiles on Key West.

Key West is the last in a long chain of islands that dangle in a graceful curve from the bottom tip of Florida; it's the farthest south you can go in the *contiguous United States*—the whole country minus Alaska and Hawaii. Instead of Cadillac Mountain's lonely gray rocks and sweet-scented pine trees, Key West boasts slim coconut palms and coral reefs darting with tropical fish. Its citizens greet the dawn with a cup of dark tropical coffee, leaning on the rails of their white-painted balconies, even while Cadillac Mountain is empty save for a few hardy hikers. But both places are waking up to the same American day.

The morning flows toward the west, and the land begins to climb up from the flat coastal plain, rumpling in rolling hills that give place in turn to a long line of mountains. Extending from the island of Newfoundland in Canada all the way south to Alabama, these are the Appalachians. Here the light glows on the mountaintops while the valleys remain in deep blue shadow. In the crisp October air, the trees lift up branches clothed in glorious oranges, reds, and golds. As they march southward, the mountains boast many different, storied names: White Mountains, Berkshires, Alleghenies, Blue Ridge Mountains, Catskills. But they are all part of the Appalachians, and they're all sharing the same American day.

Beyond the mountains, the land flattens again. To the north, the sunlight dances on the deep blue waters of the five Great Lakes: Huron, Ontario, Michigan, Erie, and Superior. They form the largest group of lakes on Earth; in fact, they contain one-fifth of all the world's fresh water. If the Great Lakes could escape their bounds, and their water were spread across the whole continent, it would cover the entire United States to a depth of five feet. Far to the south, the beautiful blue of the Great Lakes is echoed by another enormous body of water: the Gulf of Mexico. Spread between them and to the west, illuminated by the racing light, lie the Great Plains: a thousand miles of grasslands and flatlands and farms. With the morning sun climbing over the horizon, farmers rise, too, eager to bring in the October harvest. Each farm is one square in a vast checkerboard. Throughout the spring and summer, the deep, rich soil of the plains has nurtured the seeds that become corn, soybeans, and wheat. American farmers grow more corn and soybeans than anyone else in the world, here in the heart of the United States.

All this land, and all these farms, and all of the people who depend upon them: all enjoying the same American day.

Two hours after it skips past Cadillac Mountain, one hour after it greets Key West, the sunrise reaches the contiguous United States's northernmost point, an odd corner of far northern Minnesota called the Northwest Angle. It's cut off from the rest of the state, and indeed from the rest of the country, by another enormous lake—the Lake of the Woods—and it seems as though perhaps it should belong to Canada. Mostly forest, spotted with ponds and wandering deer: very few people live there. Isolated and still, it welcomes the sunrise with birdsong and the quiet murmur of tree limbs in the breeze.

Just south of the Lake of the Woods, another smaller lake lies cupped among the trees: Lake Itasca. It is an ordinary lake like thousands of others splashed across the continent, yet its quiet waters are hiding a magnificent secret, for, at one point, the lakewater tumbles over some smooth rocks and becomes a bubbling stream. This stream, tiny as it is, will grow into America's greatest river, the Mississippi, the fourth longest river in the world. From here, it unspools like a giant ribbon down the entire breadth of the United States, joined along the way by countless streams and other rivers, until, finally, in Louisiana, it spreads out into an enormous *delta* and joins the lovely turquoise waters of the Gulf of Mexico.

By now, the morning has worn itself out, and the sun rests directly overhead. It's noon, and we're in Lebanon, Kansas, a tiny town of just 60 families or so. Nothing remarkable, really— wood-sided houses, tall cottonwood trees, a main street edged with brick-fronted shops, a town like hundreds of other tiny farm towns sprinkled across the Great Plains. But our day pauses here, because Lebanon sits in the exact center of the United States. From this spot, equally in all directions, America stretches out her arms.

Beyond Lebanon, to the west, the land rises gradually, higher and drier. The checkerboard of farmland becomes less regular, and the farms themselves expand into huge ranches and gigantic wheat fields, where cattle wander and hulking tractors rumble, cutting and gathering the grain. This is the West, where the buffalo roam.

These creatures are actually American *bison*. Once, they ranged in vast herds across the whole of the Great Plains. America's largest and heaviest land animal, they wander freely through the West's wild places. Though winter is coming, and October snow is already falling in the high mountains, the bison are not concerned. They've grown thick, wooly coats that will see them through the fiercest winter blizzard.

The afternoon light finds a herd of bison in the northwestern corner of Wyoming, grazing peacefully beside a glimmering pool. But what a strange and wondrous pool: bubbling hot and wreathed in steam and ringed along its edges with rainbow-bright bands of brilliantly-colored bacteria. In the distance, a jet of boiling water erupts in a graceful arc from a mound of smooth white rock: a *geyser*. This is Yellowstone, miles and miles of wilderness set aside by American president Ulysses S. Grant in 1872 to be the world's first National Park. It is home to the nation's largest herds of bison, home as well to more than half of the world's geysers and hot springs.

A simple road winds past the bison and makes its way into the surrounding mountains, climbing upward through a shadowed forest until it levels out and crosses a bridge over a narrow lake covered with water lilies, rafts of deep green leaves, and silky yellow flowers. A wooden sign announces its name:

Isa Lake. Like Lake Itasca back in Minnesota, its quiet waters hide a secret: Isa Lake is one of the very few lakes in the entire world whose waters drain into two different oceans. It straddles the *Continental Divide*, an imaginary line that runs north and south down the great ridge of western mountains and separates the flow of water on the continent. On the eastern side of the Divide, all streams run down toward the Gulf of Mexico and the Atlantic Ocean, but on the western side all water flows toward the Pacific Ocean. The Divide runs along the Rockies, the towering mountains that rise up from the Great Plains like a mighty wall. Tracing the spine of the Rockies, the Divide makes its way south through the states of Montana, Idaho, Wyoming, Colorado, and New Mexico before continuing southward into Mexico and South America. Its central point is in the state of Colorado, where the Divide soars along the crest of many peaks taller than 13,000 feet.

But as the afternoon light plunges onward, it ricochets off the summit of a mountain that's even taller. West of the Rockies, after the land swoops down into a vast valley called the Great Basin, it climbs again in a series of jagged ridgelines: another great mountain range, the Sierra Nevadas. There, glistening with fresh October snow, stands Mt. Whitney, 14,494 feet, the contiguous United States's tallest mountain. Meanwhile, just 90 miles to the east, the evening shadows are starting to gather in Death Valley, which is America's lowest point, 282 feet below sea level.

The shadows start to spread, and streetlights come to life. The great cities of the West Coast—San Diego, Los Angeles, San Francisco, Seattle—glow like jewels. The waves of the Pacific send a greeting to California's warm, golden beaches. And far to the north, amidst the towering cedars and glassy rivers of Washington State, the sunlight bids America goodbye. It bestows a final caress on the cliff tops at Cape Flattery, the contiguous USA's northwesternmost point, and sails away over the deep blue ocean. There, as the rest of the country nestles down under the blanket of night, the sunlight will give its greetings to Alaska and Hawaii, the farthest flung of America's states.

From city to farm, from Cadillac Mountain to Mt. Whitney, from Key West to Cape Flattery, from sea to shining sea: this is a beautiful, broad country, a nation full of wonders, and it rejoices in another American day.

Chapter 2

Until 1491

The Native Americans

In fourteen hundred and ninety-two,
Columbus sailed the ocean blue.

School children across America learn this little verse: the date of the discovery of the New World and the beginning of the history of the United States.

But, of course, the land itself did not shimmer into existence in 1492. It was here long before—the big, broad, beautiful land that we saw in the last chapter—and it was filled with people.

Who were they, and how did they live here in the land before it became America?

That's not an easy question to answer, because the people who lived here before 1492 were spread widely. The countryside is huge and varied; so too were the groups of people who lived upon it deep in the past, and they did not write books telling their stories. To find them, we have to look for them in different ways: we have to seek out the footprints they left behind.

One of those faint traces can be found in what is today the state of Utah.

Far from roads or towns, a narrow canyon winds its way through the golden-red sandstone that makes up so much of the southwestern United States. The sun's heat presses heavily down on the sandy clifftops, but below, in the shadow of the canyon wall, we can find a hollow, like a cavern in the rock, with its front open to the air. There, on the rock-strewn floor, something has been constructed: a low circular wall of stones, just a foot or so high, with an opening facing toward the east, like the ghost of a door. This is the ruins of a *kiva*. When it was newly built, hundreds and hundreds of years ago, it would have been a covered room, used by its builders for ceremonies and traditions. Now it's just a shadow, a footprint left behind by those ancient Americans.

A kiva in present-day Utah

The kiva's builders were called Puebloans. They lived in the "Four Corners": that unique point in the Southwest where the states of Arizona, New Mexico, Colorado, and Utah meet. Their descendants, who still live in that region, call them the Ancient Ones. There in the desert, they built large villages—*pueblos*—using a special mixture of stone and clay called *adobe*. The structures were often several stories tall, like modern apartments, with thick, cool walls and deep-set, T-shaped doorways; for protection from enemies, they were often perched high on the sides of cliffs or atop the flat-topped mountains that are called *mesas*. One of these pueblos, at a place called Chaco Canyon in New Mexico, contained enormous houses with more than 200 rooms each, the largest buildings to be found in North America until late in the 1800s.

Pueblo cliff homes at Chaco Canyon, New Mexico

The Puebloans were expert weavers and potters and industrious farmers. The Four Corners, along with the rest of the Southwest, is a hot, dry place, and so the people of the pueblos were careful to harvest rainwater alongside their other crops. They collected the water in dammed ditches and reservoirs and clay-lined cisterns and then directed it into their fields, where they grew a plant they called *maize*, which you would recognize as corn.

For a thousand years or more, before Columbus sailed, the Puebloans lived and worked, tucked safely into their cliffside houses. In New Mexico and Arizona, people still live in the pueblos that were built by their ancestors centuries ago. For them, the footprints of the Ancient Ones are easily seen.

And there are others.

Far to the east, just across the Mississippi River from the present day city of St. Louis, Missouri, there stands a mound of earth, a flat-topped pyramid cloaked with smooth, green grass, 100 feet tall and 1,000 feet long. Around it stretches a broad park with 80 other mounds scattered here and there, the remains of a city that once covered more than six square miles. This is Cahokia, home to a people called the Mississippians. At its most prosperous, sometime in the 1200s, Cahokia might have been larger than 13th-century London.

Like the Puebloans to the southwest, the Mississippians built sprawling settlements, supporting themselves by growing crops in the fields that surrounded their cities. Instead of adobe, though, they used earth—hard-packed soil—to build their monumental structures. The mound in the center of Cahokia had been constructed by bringing dirt, one basketful at a time, and piling it up, higher and higher, over the course of many years. On the mound's flat top, the people then raised up a temple to use for the ceremonies that their religion required.

In front of the mound was a *plaza*—a large, flat, open square. Here the men played a game called *chunkey*, where two players would compete. One would roll a disc-shaped hoop of stone along the ground, and both would hurl a leather-trimmed stick, each trying to land his throw closest to the hoop as it wavered and toppled over. Enormous wagers would often be placed on these games. The winner would be celebrated; the loser forfeited all he had, including, sometimes, his life.

You can see the remains of Cahokia today should you ever visit St. Louis. Perhaps you can hear the echoes of the shouting spectators, cheering their favorite at a chunkey match. The mound at Cahokia, huge as it is, is a footprint left by the past.

And, still, there are others.

Further to the east, in the very southernmost part of Ohio, you can find another immense mound, this one 1,400 feet long, formed in the shape of a long, coiling serpent, and so called The Serpent Mound.

The Serpent Mound in present-day Ohio

In the Colorado Desert in California, ancient Americans carved giant pictures—men, animals, spiral shapes—directly into the dry ground by removing the dark layer of soil on the surface to reveal the pale rock underneath. High in the mountains of Wyoming, a great wheel of rocks now called the Bighorn Medicine Wheel has been carefully laid out so that its spokes align with the winter and summer solstices. And if we go back to that quiet canyon in Utah, we'll find the walls decorated with little pictures—pictographs—perhaps left there by the same Ancient Ones who built the kiva.

The Bighorn Medicine Wheel in present-day Wyoming

Of course, as time passed, the lives and ways of all of these people gradually changed. The city of Cahokia was abandoned, sometime in the mid-14th century, after being deluged by Mississippi River floods. The people who lived in the pueblos of Chaco Canyon faced the opposite problem: a 50-year-long drought that made it impossible for them to continue to survive in their dry canyon-lands. They moved away, joining other peoples to the north or west, adapting to the change in their circumstances as best they could.

And so, in every corner of this land, from the coasts of the Atlantic to the far Pacific shore, from the forests of the north to the grasslands of the Plains, people lived and worked and farmed and played. They made war on one another; they traded food and crafts with one another; they married and reared children; they mourned their dead. Across the years and miles, they shared many of the same beliefs: respect the elderly, live together in communities, stay true to tradition, tend the land and defend it from enemies. They were the first Americans, the *Native* Americans.

These people were grouped into *tribes*: groups that live in the same region or share the same language. A tribe, in turn, might be part of a larger *nation* or be divided up into smaller *clans*, which are family groups. Each tribe had its own name for itself and its own way of living.

In the northeast, in the boundless woodlands that surround the Great Lakes and the rivers that flow into the Atlantic, the tribes built their homes close to the water. They used the trees' bark, both for small things like bowls and cups and also to craft graceful canoes. Even their houses were made from bark, layered skillfully over frames made from flexible young trees. Some of these bark houses were small and round, called *wigwams,* and some of them were truly enormous: *longhouses* that stretched for 200 feet or more, with ceilings 25 feet high. These would be divided up, inside, with walls made from colorful blankets; each family in the longhouse would have its own space. Bonfires burned along the center, with the smoke escaping through holes in the roof. A longhouse would be measured by the number of fires it could contain. A 12-fire house was a large home, indeed.

The forest provided them with all they needed. They hunted deer, fished for trout and eels, and gathered mussels and oysters from the ocean. They used polished shells to make beads, a craft they called *wampum*; these they traded with other tribes further inland for furs and corn. When their work was done, they played games, including a fast and wild sport that involved tossing a small ball into the air and catching and passing it with long, netted sticks; today, many people still enjoy this game, which we now call *lacrosse.*

To the south, in the lowlands and gentle hills, the early descendants of Cahokia's mound builders continued to be skilled farmers. Like many other tribes, they grew the "Three Sisters": corn, beans, and squash. The corn would be planted first in a little hill with a piece of rotted fish as fertilizer. When the corn had begun to sprout and grow, the bean and squash seeds would be added. The beans could then twine themselves around the corn, using the tall stalks for support, and the squash vines would spread around the mound, keeping the ground cool and moist. Planting this way allowed the farmers to grow as much food as they possibly could in a single field. Corn was vastly important, so much so that the Natives of the southeast marked the start of each new year by the ripening of the first ears of corn.

Their houses were built from wooden poles and planks that were plastered securely with mud. Farther south, where the land was wet and even swampy, the people constructed their houses on raised platforms so that they could stay comfortable and dry and perhaps catch a cooling breeze in the evenings.

They hunted, too: deer, rabbits, and even, in the farthest parts of the southeast, alligators.

To the west, in the great stretch of plains, Native Americans were less tied to specific patches of ground. They moved from place to place, following the enormous herds of bison that roamed the grasslands. The bison provided them with all the things that the northeastern Natives gained from trees: clothing, shoes, and shelter made from hides; knives, cups, bowls, and needles made from bone.

Their shelters were called *teepees:* a kind of tent made of bison skins sewn together. This covering was arranged over a tall frame created by leaning five poles against each other and tying them together at the top. Each teepee was furnished with a low, round door, which was usually pointed toward the east so that the teepee faced the sunrise. The teepee was cool and dry in the summer and warm and snug in the winter. A small fire would be set burning at its center, and the smoke would drift out the top through a skillfully-engineered flap.

The Natives of the Plains could pack up their teepee villages whenever the bison moved or whenever the weather grew harsh. They roamed back and forth easily across the Great Plains, measuring their year by the seasons. They started each new year's calendar on the day of the first snowfall.

In the northwest, along the cool, green coastline of the Pacific, the people marked the seasons differently. They looked for the return of the salmon, a fish that swims far out in the ocean for most of the year until its instincts call it home, in the fall, back to the stream where it was born. As the salmon returned each fall, the people of the northwestern coasts captured them with nets and baskets and then smoked and dried the fish to feed themselves throughout the year to come. They added to their storehouse of food, like so many of the other first Americans, with skilled hunting. Their prey was found in the ocean: otters, seals, and even whales. Unlike the Plains people, these Natives of the northwest lived in permanent houses, with fires along the center like the longhouses far to the east. These homes were built of sweet-smelling wood from cedar trees, with the tall ceilings often held aloft by totem poles. Each totem pole was a single large log, stripped of its bark and branches and carved and painted with animals of all sorts, some of them fantastical like the thunderbird, a mythical creature whose billowing wings they believed caused the deafening clap of the thunderstorm. Many families would live in one such house, and they celebrated important days by inviting another household to join them in a special kind of feast: a *potlatch,* where the host of the feast would give gifts to everyone who attended.

This was America: bark canoes and bison hides, teepees and wigwams, longhouses and pueblos. The people living as they had for hundreds of years, no doubt assuming that life would continue much as it always had.

But it wouldn't.

A change was coming, an astounding change, coming from across the sea, sailing toward them on a new tide, in the year fourteen hundred and ninety-two.

Chapter 3

Toscanelli's Map

Sail West to Reach the East

In the year 1474, in the city of Florence, which lies right near the center of Italy's boot, a scholar named Paolo Toscanelli had drawn a map of the world.

Since his youth, Toscanelli had been interested in geography, the study of the earth's surface. He had sought out stories from sailors and travelers; he had studied the writings of the ancient Greek philosophers and tested with his own mathematics their estimations of the size of the globe. He had read a book written almost 200 years earlier by the explorer and merchant Marco Polo, who described his journeys in far-off Asia. He exchanged letters with other scholars, discussing the Earth's distant reaches. Slowly, over the years, as he thought about all of this, Toscanelli came to a startling conclusion: if a person wanted to follow in the footsteps of Marco Polo and travel to the lands of the East— and in 1474 there were many who wanted very much to do just that, for reasons that we shall see—perhaps that person should board a ship and sail boldly out into the ocean, not eastward, but to the west, instead.

But wait, you might be asking, how can that be? Surely east and west are opposites, and thus forever separate from one another! How can you reach the East by sailing west?

The answer, of course, lies in the fact that the earth is a sphere, which Toscanelli, like most of the educated men of his day, knew very well. Since the time of the ancient Greeks, who used shadow and light to measure the curve of the earth's surface, people had been aware of the world's roundness; they had known, too, that there were three parts to it—Africa, Asia, and Europe—and that these continents were cradled on all sides by the great "Ocean Sea."

If you study your globe and put one finger on China and the other on Italy's boot, you can see how Marco Polo would have needed to travel toward the east to get from Italy to China. But suppose he had sailed off to the west, instead? If you trace your finger to the west, all the long way around, eventually you'll come to China that way, too. That's how the west can bring you, eventually, to the east.

Toscanelli created a map to illustrate this idea. He plotted it carefully, drawing the outlines of the three parts of the known world: he put Europe on the map's right side, with Africa below it, and then, off to the left, to the west, the wondrous lands of Asia: Cathay, which we know today as China; India, with a spray of islands scattered before it; and the then-fabled Cipango, the island of Japan. When he was satisfied with it, he copied it carefully onto a fresh sheet of parchment, packaged it up, and sent it off to Alfonso V, king of Portugal, along with a letter urging the king to give the idea his careful consideration. "Be not amazed," he cautioned, "if I call west [the place] where the spice grows, for it is commonly said that it grows in the east, yet whoso steers west will always find the said parts in the west, and whoso goes east overland will find the same parts in the east." Whether you travel east or west, he was saying, you will eventually arrive in Asia.

Toscanelli knew that King Alfonso would be intrigued by the possibility of a new western route to Asia. In the year 1474, when Toscanelli had completed his map, getting to Asia had become very troublesome.

In centuries past, throughout the long years of the Middle Ages, travelers such as Marco Polo made their way into Asia by following the Silk Road: a long, well-trodden way that stretched from the easternmost parts of Europe and the Mediterranean Sea; through Turkey and along the northern reaches of Persia and India; and across the entire length of China, to the city of Shanghai on China's eastern coast. For over a thousand years, since before the birth of Jesus and the fall of Rome, this road had been the gateway for trade, through which the people of Europe had been able to acquire the riches of Asia: soft silk fabric, sweet-smelling woods, glossy porcelain bowls, smooth white paper, rich black tea, fossilized amber and gleaming pearls, and, most of all, spices. The Silk Road carried with it the scent of cinnamon and nutmeg, pepper and clove, all of them grown far to the east, mostly on islands off the coasts of India and China.

Now, of course, you know these spices if you've ever dipped a fork into a slice of pumpkin pie after Thanksgiving dinner or drunk a cup of ginger tea on a cold winter evening. But, for Europeans in the 1400s, the importance of spice went far beyond mere deliciousness. In those days, long before the invention of electricity and refrigerators, keeping food fresh and sweet was a mighty struggle. Spices helped the food taste better, even if it were on the edge of spoiling, and so the cooks used spices in every dish: meats, fruits, vegetables, desserts. Even wine and beer were spiced with pepper and nutmeg. People would chew cinnamon and licorice root to freshen their breath and clean their teeth in the same way you might reach for a toothbrush and a tube of toothpaste. Spices were used as medicine, too, to combat coughing fits and upset stomachs and painful bruises. For the wealthy, a dining table adorned with bowls of mounded spices was a sign of high status, because the spices were expensive and rare and had traveled such a long way. Spices were so desirable that, during the Middle Ages, pepper or nutmeg could be used as a substitute for money, and landlords would accept spices as payment for rent or taxes. A baron in England, in his cold stone castle, would feel a little warmer as he drank his nutmeg-spiced wine.

The Silk Road made that possible.

But, in 1453, the mighty city of Constantinople, which had stood unbowed since the days of the Roman Empire, fell to its enemies. Its conquerors were the Ottoman Turks; they were followers of a religion called Islam, with which the Christian nations of Europe had been at war, off and on, for 500 years. The new masters of Constantinople charged enormous taxes to any European merchant or traveler wishing to travel through their lands on the Silk Road, making the luxurious goods of Asia, which were already expensive, suddenly much more so. Few of the merchants were willing to pay such high prices, and travel and trade between Europe and Asia abruptly declined. It became very difficult to acquire nutmeg for the wine.

Of course, the merchants and traders of Europe, along with all of Europe's kings, were determined to find a way around the Turks—some kind of back door to Asia. Perhaps, if not by land on the Silk Road, they could go by sea? They began looking thoughtfully to the south, to Africa. Might a brave man be able to sail down along Africa's coast and find a route around its uncharted length and so make his way to India and China and the Spice Islands? After all, Africa couldn't be endless, could it?

It was at this point, with these musings weighing on his mind, that King Alfonso of Portugal received Toscanelli's map.

King Alfonso considered it: Could this be the back door to Asia that all of Europe was looking for? Could one reach the East by sailing out to the west, across the vast and unknown Atlantic, the mysterious Ocean Sea? A fascinating idea, to be sure, but no one had ever heard news of any sailor accomplishing such a feat. The kingdom of Portugal sits like a mask on the face of Spain, looking out over the Atlantic's green waters and beyond. Past that western horizon, no one knew what dangers might await, and the ships of Portugal, though they ventured far, tended to stay within an easy distance of the shore. In any case, surely such a journey—straight out across the ocean, to the far side of the world—would take too long. No ship could carry enough food and water to sustain its crew across this immense distance! Perhaps it would be more sensible to hold fast to their previous plan: sail down the coast of Africa and try to find a way around its southern tip. Atlantic or Africa? West or South? Alfonso considered and met with his advisors, and they long debated the question.

But, as they debated, the map and the ideas it contained became known to someone else: a sailor from Genoa, Italy, named Cristoforo Columbo. We know him today by his English name: Christopher Columbus. He was very intrigued by Toscanelli's map, because he had his own ambitions about reaching Asia, his own secret ideas about finding a new route, and they both involved sailing out, far out, into the ocean blue.

Chapter 4

Searching for Cipango

The Voyage of Christopher Columbus

Christopher Columbus

Christopher Columbus had been a sailor from his youth. He was born in 1451 in Genoa, a town in Italy, one of three sons born to a weaver named Domenico Columbo and his wife, Susanna; but Christopher left his family behind, perhaps when he was as young as 10 years old, and took to the sea. He worked as a cabin boy, running errands for the ship's captain. After several years of this lowly labor, he became a full-fledged crewman and voyaged numerous times across the Mediterranean

Sea, along the coasts of North Africa and to Greece. By 1477, his home port was Lisbon, the principal city of Portugal. His thirst for travel grew ever stronger, and soon he was working aboard ships that ventured farther out on the Atlantic Ocean to France and England. Some say that he went as far north as Iceland, the land that the ancients had labeled Ultima Thule, "the farthest point," because to them it seemed like the very end of the world.

He sailed south, too, toward Spain's Canary Islands, which lie in the ocean about 60 miles west of North Africa. There, he saw for himself the Canary Current, a river of faster-flowing water within the ocean itself, streaming off toward the west. There, also, he heard tales of strange things—carved gourds, small wooden statues—that had washed up on the island beaches, objects that must have come from lands far away. Is it any wonder that he began to look to the far horizon, dreaming of what lay beyond it?

So, with his years of sailing experience, Columbus must have been intrigued when he learned of Toscanelli's map and the plan it contained for reaching the East by sailing west across the Atlantic. He wrote to Toscanelli at once, asking: Is such a journey really possible?

Toscanelli's response was quick and assured: "The voyage is not only possible," he wrote in his answer to Columbus's letter, "but it is true, and certain to be honorable and to yield incalculable profit, and very great fame among all Christians." He encouraged Columbus to try, saying, "I do not wonder that you, who have great courage, should with a burning heart feel a great desire to undertake the voyage."

But, of course, it is not such a simple thing to undertake a voyage! Crewmen, supplies, and, most of all, ships must be had: outfitting an expedition of this size would require an enormous amount of money and influence, neither of which Columbus possessed. He needed a *patron:* someone to supply the funds for the voyage who would then receive in return most of the profits.

And, for a journey this ambitious, Columbus must have the support of someone not only rich but also powerful, someone whose authority over land and sea would be unquestioned. He needed a king.

He went first to Portugal. By now it was 1484, and a new king, John II, sat on the throne. He listened to Columbus's proposal and then presented it to his council for their advice. After deliberating for a few days, the council rejected Columbus's idea. They told the king that Columbus was quite mistaken in his estimations of the distance involved. It was too far; it was not possible for any ship to carry enough supplies for the journey. No, they said, forget this Columbus fellow! Portugal must hold fast to its current plan: They would reach Asia by sailing south around the tip of Africa. Bowing to this advice, John II sent Columbus away empty-handed.

Undeterred, Columbus decided to try Spain instead. The rulers there were a king and a queen: Ferdinand and Isabella. They, too, sent Columbus to one of their councils, and that council answered Columbus with the same doleful words: The journey he was proposing was simply too far. The Ocean Sea was too large to cross. It was impossible.

Two more years dragged by as Columbus wearily sought a patron to pay for his expedition. He even sent his brother, Bartholomew, to England in the hopes of interesting the English king, Henry VII. But Bartholomew's ship and all aboard were captured by pirates; many more months passed while they struggled to free themselves and complete the journey to London.

And so, in January of 1492, Columbus appealed to Isabella and Ferdinand one last time. Just as before, they were unconvinced and dismissed him. But, as he rode away, determined never again to approach them, one of their councilors intervened with the king and queen. If we turn Columbus away, he said, he will surely find a different royal patron. What of the immense fortune that might be gained by finding this new route to Asia? Would we want such wealth to enrich another nation when we could have it for Spain? Wasn't the possibility of enormous profits worth the risk?

After a moment, the king and queen agreed and sent a messenger to fetch Columbus back. He would have *letters patent*, they told him, which would give him the right to claim land, to establish treaties, and to trade, all in the name of the Spanish crown. Along with that, they granted him money to buy supplies, to hire a crew, and to *commandeer* some ships. Columbus would cross the wide Atlantic to Asia under the flag of Ferdinand and Isabella!

On August 3rd, 1492, Columbus sailed away from Spain in command of three ships. The largest, the *Santa Maria*, measured perhaps 90 feet long; the other two were called the *Niña* and the *Pinta,* and they were much smaller. One hundred men or so made up the expedition's crew, and Columbus's journals tell us that not one of those hundred was eager to be there. As a foreigner from Italy, Columbus had struggled to recruit Spanish sailors for a mission into the frightening, unknown Ocean Sea. In the end, it was the captain of the *Pinta*, a Spaniard named Martín Alonso Pinzón, who persuaded many of his fellow countrymen to join the crew.

On board their small vessels, the men had little room to roam. There were no cabins, no berths, no hammocks, no galleys. The men slept out on the deck, often tying themselves down to avoid rolling overboard at night. During the day, they sang, whittled, gambled, and grumbled. None of them were convinced that Columbus knew where he was going.

But Columbus was certain. At his right hand, as he stood at the wheel of the *Santa Maria*, was Toscanelli's map.

At first, they were sailing through known waters, south toward Africa and then west to the Canary Islands. Columbus remembered the Canary Current, and he planned to use it to speed them westward. After they departed the Canaries on

September 6, each day saw them farther from the known world, sailing toward the setting sun, pulled along by the current and the promise of Asia's riches.

By mid-September, they began to see signs of life in the water: leaves and branches that must have come from land and a kind of drifting seaweed that only grows in shallow seas. On September 25, a flare of excitement blazed through the crew at the sight of gray shadows on the far horizon. Could it be land? But, alas, it was only low banks of clouds. Gloom and fear descended once more, only to be relieved on October 7, when joyous shouts erupted from the crew as they spotted flocks of birds wheeling low over the waves. Surely, this could only mean that land was near!

Midnight of October 11 found them sailing under a bright, moonlit sky. Peering forward, as always, Columbus was startled to see lights, sparkling for a moment at the furthest edge of sight. Two hours later, in the early morning hours of October 12, 1492, a lookout stationed far up in the *Pinta's* rigging shouted at the top of his lungs: *Tierra! Tierra!*

Land!

The light of dawn revealed to them a low island, garlanded with beaches of gleaming white sand. Columbus noted that "the island is rather large and very flat, with bright green trees, much water, and a very large lake in the center, without any mountain, and the whole land so green that it is a pleasure to look on it." As Columbus and Captain Pinzón set foot on shore, after 36 days at sea, they carried the royal banner of Ferdinand and Isabella. Columbus planted it firmly in the sand and called out for Captain Pinzón to witness that he had taken possession of this island for the king and queen of Portugal. Columbus called the land San Salvador, which means "Holy Savior," in order to give glory to God for his successful voyage.

Although Columbus claimed this island for his sovereigns, it was not an empty place. Soon, curious about these strange visitors, the island's inhabitants left their hiding places among the trees and came forward to greet them. Columbus described them as "a very handsome people" with "beautiful eyes" and "good countenances." They were friendly and generous, willingly trading their island's riches—fluttering parrots, balls of spun thread, spears—for glass beads and red sailor's caps as they introduced their land to Columbus.

But what land was it? Looking back from our vantage point in history, we know that Columbus landed on one of the islands known today as the Bahamas, in the Caribbean Sea. From that island beach, the whole vast continent of North America stretched up to the north, to the west lay Mexico and Central America, and to the southwest, the jungles and deserts and mountains of South America.

Columbus, however, thought otherwise.

The friendly people he called *los indios*, which is "the Indians" in the Spanish language, because he was certain that he had accomplished what Toscanelli had predicted with his map: he had sailed west across the Atlantic Ocean to the spice islands of India, the rich and fabled East. He was brimful of excitement and impatient to leave this small island behind. Later, in his journal entry for October 13th, he wrote that, despite his pleasure in the lovely place he'd found, "in order not to lose time, I intend to go and see if I can find the island of Cipango."

Cipango, you might remember, was labeled on Toscanelli's map; it was another name for Japan. Columbus was convinced that he had voyaged to Asia, and he would maintain that certainty for the rest of his life.

For the next few months, the three ships wandered around the Caribbean Sea, searching for Cipango. They explored the islands that we know today as Cuba and Hispaniola where, on Christmas Day, the *Santa Maria* ran aground. Leaving some men behind to build a fort and establish themselves, Columbus loaded the rest of the *Santa Maria*'s crew aboard the *Niña* and the *Pinta* and turned eastward toward home, sailing for Spain on January 16, 1493. After a dreadful voyage beset with storms, which separated him from the *Pinta*, Columbus and the *Niña* sighted the Spanish coast on March 15.

What a welcome they received! They had accomplished something that had been considered impossible: They had shown that the vast Ocean Sea could be crossed after all. They had sailed west to Asia!

Except, of course, they hadn't.

It would remain for someone else, as we shall see in the next chapter, to realize the true nature of Columbus's voyage: he had sailed—not to Cipango, not to Cathay, but instead to an entirely New World.

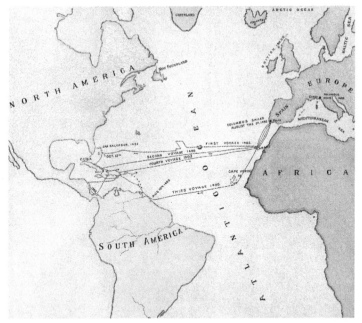

Columbus's Voyages to the New World

Chapter 5

The Fourth Part of the World

John Cabot and Amerigo Vespucci

L ike Columbus, the men of Bristol were certain that land
existed to the west.

Bristol is perched on the southwestern coast of England,
near the mouth of the River Avon. It is a port city, which means
that its shoreline is edged with docks where ships can be moored
and cargo loaded. Bristol had always been home to men of the
sea who ventured far out into the Atlantic Ocean in search of
fish and also in search of a wonder: a magical island called Hy-
Brasil.

Legends told of a land far to the west, an island eternally
cloaked in mist but for one day every seven years when the fog
would lift and the land could be seen but never touched. It was
a circular island pierced through the center with a rushing river,
green as paradise and sparkling with dew. In 1480 and again in
1481, just 11 years before Columbus sailed, the men of Bristol
set out to seek for Hy-Brasil. When they returned, they insisted
that they'd seen land on the distant horizon. The ocean did not
stretch out endlessly. Something was out there.

They weren't the first ones to entertain that suspicion.
Five hundred years earlier, a band of men from Norway had
embarked on a voyage to the west under the leadership of an

adventurer named Leif Erikson. They were aiming for the enormous island that today we call Greenland, but a storm blew them off course, and instead they reached a rocky shore, a land filled with meadows of grain and grapevines. They called it "Vinland" and built a small settlement. But the native people who lived there were fierce, and eventually Leif Erickson and his men abandoned Vinland and sailed back to Greenland, never to return. Only their story lingered, told and retold by seafaring men.

The men of Bristol were unsurprised, then, when an Italian sailor arrived in their city in the year 1496, bearing a letter with the king's seal that authorized him to seek for land in the west. His name was Giovanni Caboto, but the Englishmen called him John Cabot.

He was a born traveler, a citizen of Venice, that beautiful city in Italy threaded with canals and filled with mariners, but he had moved to Spain by 1492. Along with every Spanish sailor, he had read Columbus's descriptions of his travels; he was eager to build upon what Columbus had done. He studied his globe, and he reasoned that, if one were to begin his voyage from a point farther north, the journey to the west might be shortened. This is because the more toward the north one goes in *latitude*, the closer together the lines of *longitude*.

An understanding of latitude and longitude is necessary for *navigation*, for finding your way on the vast and featureless ocean. Latitude and longitude are a system of imaginary lines laid out on the surface of the earth. If you examine a globe, you'll see those lines printed out, skimming across both land and water. The lines of latitude run parallel to the *equator*, which circles the earth's middle like a belt. The lines of longitude run north and south, in rings that meet together at the North and South Poles. Together, the lines of latitude and longitude cross each other to form squares that can define the position of any place on earth. As you study your globe, you might notice that, as you travel northward, the lines of latitude remain the same distance from each other, but the lines of longitude draw closer and closer together, finally merging at the North Pole. This was the observation that occurred to John Cabot: if someone were to sail at a more northerly latitude, where the lines of longitude were closer together, surely the distance across the Ocean Sea would be shorter.

So, in 1495, Cabot came to England, hoping to win support for an English voyage to the west. He went to London first, and there he met an Italian friar, a priest of the Roman Catholic Church, who happened to be acquainted personally with England's king, Henry VII. He offered to arrange an introduction for Cabot.

This was fortunate, indeed, for both men. Cabot needed men and ships and supplies; Henry VII wanted a part in any new trade route to Asia so that all of the potential wealth did not rest solely in the hands of Ferdinand and Isabella of Spain. When John Cabot explained his plans, Henry VII at once bestowed on him *letters patent,* much like the Spanish monarchs had given to Columbus. They granted John Cabot free authority to sail to all coasts of the eastern, western, and northern sea, "under our banners" to find and investigate "whatsoever islands, countries, regions or provinces of heathens and infidels, in whatsoever part of the world placed, which before this time were unknown to all Christians."

So, with the power of the king behind him, John Cabot came to Bristol, his son Sebastian by his side. The king had specified that he was to sail from the port there, since the men of Bristol were famed as explorers themselves; their search for Hy-Brasil well-known. From among the ships gathered at Bristol's docks, Cabot chose a small, fast, sea-worthy vessel, and, in the spring of 1496, he set out. But this first voyage was a disaster: his crew defied his orders; his supplies ran low; and terrible, sweeping storms battered his ship. Discouraged, he turned back after just a few weeks.

The next year, in 1497, he tried again. His new ship, the *Matthew*, was equipped with supplies for seven or eight months of travel, a crew of 20 men, and a barber from Italy invited along not to give haircuts but to be the ship's surgeon. They sailed away from Bristol's port on a morning in May.

Several weeks later, having navigated ever westward with the North Star at his right hand, John Cabot and the crew of the *Matthew* spied land ahead. They dropped anchor on the morning of June 24 and carefully examined the shore. It was deserted, but they could see signs of people: a net, the remains of a bonfire, wooden tools, and a trail made by human feet. Cautiously, careful never to go farther inland than the distance that a crossbow could *shoot a bolt*, they ventured ashore and planted the banner of Henry VII, establishing England's claim to this land. They replenished their supply of fresh water and reboarded the *Matthew*. Slowly, over the next days and weeks, they made their way along the coastline. Many years later, John Cabot's son, Sebastian, described the land they saw:

> *The people of it are dressed in the skins of animals. They use in their wars bows and arrows, lances and darts, and certain clubs of wood, and slings. It is a very sterile land. There are in it many white bears, and very large stags* like horses, *and many other animals; and likewise there is infinite fish.* . . . *There are in the same land hawks black as crows, eagles, partridges,* linnets, *and many other kinds of birds of different species.*

There were fish, too, in shoals, or large schools, so thick and vast that the ships could not pass through them. They were able to catch all that they could possibly eat by simply lowering baskets into the water.

By mid-July, they were sailing back toward Bristol, arriving in port on August 6th. The men of Bristol duly recorded the tale of their travels in the city's history, but of course they, the voyagers of Bristol, had known all along that there was land out there. Had they not seen it themselves, in the years past, when they had gone questing for the legendary island of Hy-Brasil?

King Henry VII was pleased indeed that his royal banner had been planted on such far shores. This gave England a claim to any trade that would happen between Europe and Asia along this new route. The king awarded Cabot with money and honor, and it was soon reported that he walked about in London dressed in silk and was addressed as "Lord Admiral." He also received from the king permission to mount another expedition to this "New Found Land," taking 300 men with him. This time, he assured the king, he would press even farther to the west, and he would surely find Cipango, succeeding where Columbus had failed. The 300 men would build an outpost, and into it all the wealth of Asia could flow and from there back across the sea to England. London, Cabot claimed, would be a "greater depot of spices than there is in Alexandria." England would be very rich indeed.

But it was not to be.

The new expedition departed from Bristol in May of 1498 with five ships, all of them stuffed with the goods of England— woolen cloth, fine lace, well-sewn caps—intended to be traded for the spices of Asia. One of the ships was caught in a storm and forced to limp back to Bristol, but the other four sailed onward.

They were never seen again, and no news of them ever returned to England. Like the mythical Hy-Brasil, they vanished into the mist, possibly lost at sea. And Henry VII, who was soon to be caught up in wars with France, turned his attention away from exploration. The land that John Cabot had found was, for a little while, forgotten by the English.

But what was this land? Columbus's Indies, Leif Erickson's Vinland, John Cabot's New Found Land?

Both Columbus and Cabot went to their deaths certain that they had discovered a new route to Asia and that the lands they had seen were islands off the coast of India or China. But we know now that they were no such thing. What these two had found was an entire continent, hitherto unsuspected by anyone in Europe. A new world, a fourth part of the world to add to the three—Europe, Africa, Asia—that they already knew. The journeys of Columbus and Cabot had made the world a far larger place, even if they themselves never realized this.

Why, then, was this New World not christened "Columbia" or "Cabota" to honor either of them?

The answer to that question takes us back to Paolo Toscanelli and his map.

Toscanelli was a man with many friends, among whom was a man named Giorgio Antonio Vespucci, a scholar and priest celebrated throughout Italy as the most learned of men. This Giorgio had a nephew whom he was helping to educate: Amerigo Vespucci. The young Amerigo had studied a copy of Toscanelli's map and perhaps even discussed it with his uncle's friend. When Columbus returned from his journey and declared his intention of setting out again on a second voyage, Amerigo Vespucci was given the task of outfitting Columbus's ships with supplies. By the end of the 1490s, he had made two voyages himself to the "Indies" that Columbus had found.

But Amerigo was a highly educated, accomplished geographer, and he began to have doubts. The animals, the people, the trees: none of it matched any description of Asia that he had ever read. It was something different, something new. In a letter written after he returned to Spain, he said,

> *It is lawful to call it a new world, because none of these countries were known to our ancestors, and to all who hear*

about them they will be entirely new. . . . It was on the 7th of August 1501, that we reached those countries, thanking our Lord God with solemn prayers, and celebrating a choral Mass. We knew that land to be a continent, and not an island.

And, of course, he was entirely correct.

Amerigo's letters describing his voyages to this New World were copied and recopied and quickly spread throughout Europe. A mapmaker in Germany, upon reading them, was inspired to create a new map, with the new continent included for the first time, and, to honor Amerigo Vespucci, he wrote "America" across the top; over the years, the name remained.

America, the new land, the Fourth Part of the World.

No longer hidden, no longer unsuspected, but still unknown, if only for a little while longer.

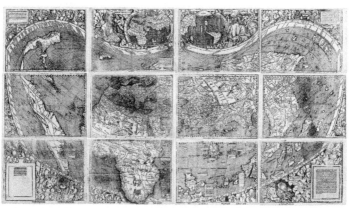

Map of the New World created by Martin Waldseemüller in 1507

Chapter 6

Bold Spaniards

Conquistadors and Explorers

Have you ever thought about how a path is formed? At first, there is nothing but softly blowing grass and tangled weeds. But if someone wanders through, he'll leave behind the marks of his passage, and, if another person wishes to go that way, he will follow in the first fellow's steps. Soon, as more and more walkers trace that same trail, it becomes defined and clear: a solid, dusty pathway formed by the tramping of many feet.

In the same manner, after Columbus had first shown the way, others came after him. The king of Spain, who had sent Columbus on his journey, saw the newly-blazed trail shining like a torch, beckoning others to follow and do as Columbus had done. The king encouraged them to go, especially when it became clear that Amerigo Vespucci was correct and this was a new and unknown continent, a huge land filled with the possibility of boundless treasures. In 1494, King Ferdinand signed an agreement with the King of Portugal: the Treaty of Tordesillas. In it, the two rulers divided between them these newly-discovered lands. And so it was that, in the years following Columbus's first voyage in 1492, many Spaniards boldly ventured out into the

New World, eager to discover, to survey, and to gain what wealth they could for their king and also for themselves.

They were called *conquistadors*—conquerors—because they came both to explore the land in search of gold and to conquer its people in the name of King Ferdinand. They followed Columbus's path to the islands in the Caribbean Sea, and then from there they went farther onward, into every part of the Americas: North, Central, and South.

One of them, Juan Ponce de León, founded a *colony* on the large island that today we call Puerto Rico. He built a large estate, mostly—alas—by forcing the natives into slavery and making them work for him day and night. But then he quarreled bitterly over the governorship of the island with Diego, son of Christopher Columbus, and decided to leave Puerto Rico behind and explore farther to the west. Bearing King Ferdinand's blessing, Ponce de León set off on March 4, 1513, with three ships and 200 men. A few weeks later, on April 2, Ponce de León and his ships spotted a huge swath of land—an enormous island, they thought—which he claimed for the king. He named it *La Florida*, because it was the Easter season, the time of year that the Spanish called the Festival of Flowers.

On they sailed, southward along the green and lovely coast, until they found islands ringed with coral reefs—the long chain of isles swinging off the tip of Florida that we now call the Keys. They threaded their way through and made their way north, with the land on their right hand, now, beautiful land covered with low, rounded *hummocks* of mangrove trees and tall, moss-strewn cypresses. The beaches were white as salt and soft as silk.

Later, legends would claim that Ponce de León was searching for a Fountain of Youth, a clear, flowing spring whose waters could give a man eternal life. But, in truth, he and his men were seeking treasure. Always, always, they looked for gold, but they found none. They did find native people, some of whom were friendly and some who were most decidedly not. The land flowed on endlessly, and Ponce de León realized that this was no mere island. It must be part of the larger continent.

At last, after a voyage that lasted eight months, they were forced by lack of supplies to turn and make their way back toward Puerto Rico. Ponce de León then hurried to Spain to personally report to King Ferdinand and gain from him a *charter*—a document giving him permission to build a Spanish colony in La Florida. In 1521 he sailed again to that beautiful land with men and horses and enough tools and supplies to construct a settlement. But it was not to be; the Natives who lived near their chosen site were not willing to accept these interlopers. They attacked with spears and bows, and Ponce de León was pierced through the thigh with a poisoned arrow. The colony was abandoned, and the ships sailed away to Cuba, where Ponce de León died of his wound.

But his were another set of footprints along the trail that Columbus pioneered, and others were soon to follow.

In 1510, a man named Vasco Nuñez de Balboa established the first settlement on the mainland of the Americas, in the land that we now call Colombia. From there he ventured farther west, across the narrow neck—the *isthmus*—of Panama, and there became, in 1513, the first European to see the huge expanse of the Pacific Ocean. After him came a man named Hernán Cortés, who landed on the shores of Mexico in 1519 with 500 men on 11 ships. Legend says that he sunk all of the ships but one so that his men had no choice but to press onward toward conquest with no thought of retreat. And conquer they did; Mexico at that time was ruled by the vast and powerful Aztec Empire, but the Aztec were defeated nonetheless by Cortés and his men. To the south, in what is now Peru and Chile, the empire of the Inca was likewise brought low by the conquistador Francisco Pizzaro.

In May of 1539, another Spaniard landed in Florida with more than 600 men, nine ships, 237 horses, and 200 pigs. His name was Hernando de Soto. He had been a lieutenant of

Pizzaro's during his conquest of the Inca, but, desiring to strike out on his own, he had petitioned the king to give him the right to explore and colonize La Florida, since Ponce de León was dead. He fully expected to take all of North America for Spain; he estimated that this task would require a mere four years.

But, like all of the conquistadors, de Soto was more interested in gold than in settlements. Instead of staying put in Florida and establishing farms and towns, he moved ever onward, farther and farther north. He traveled all the way up Florida's *peninsula* and then wandered for hundreds of miles through the lands that are now the states of Georgia, South Carolina, North Carolina, Tennessee, and Alabama. It was in Alabama that trouble found him, for there he ended up in pitched battle with the native people who lived there. Many of his men were killed. He burned the Natives' town by way of vengeance, killing many of them in return, but by then his expedition had lost almost all of its supplies and a quarter of its horses. With his remaining men, he limped west, across Alabama and into Mississippi. Here they encountered another native tribe, the Chickasaw. De Soto demanded that they give him 200 men as slaves to carry what remained of their supplies, but, perhaps unsurprisingly, the Chickasaws attacked. All of de Soto's remaining equipment was destroyed, and 40 more men were killed.

Fleeing the Chickasaws, with the bright lure of gold still filling his eyes, de Soto and his remaining men forged westward. In May of 1541, they came upon a wonder: a river so broad and smooth, so stupendously huge, that they were struck speechless. It was what we now call the Mississippi River. If you have ever seen it or crossed over it on an immense bridge, you might understand how they felt.

For de Soto, the river, though magnificent, was an enormous obstacle. There were no bridges in those days! How could he possibly cross? In the end, he and his men spent a month building rafts, hiding from bands of foraging natives; they slipped across the river late one night under cover of darkness. They continued traveling—through Arkansas, Oklahoma, and Texas.

Strangely, although de Soto did not know it, another Spanish expedition was also roaming through North America at exactly the same time. Less than 200 miles away, a group led by a man named Francisco Vázquez de Coronado was making its way through Kansas, having spent many months scouring the American Southwest searching for cities made of gold.

This Coronado had been a governor of a Spanish province in Mexico, since, now that Spain had conquered that land, they needed men to rule it. But Coronado had heard rumors of a place far to the north called Cibola with seven cities of gold: streets paved with gold and houses built of golden bricks. The idea of such wealth seized Coronado's imagination, and, at his own great expense, he outfitted an expedition and journeyed north out of Mexico, following the Zuni River, which led him up into Arizona. There, by capturing and questioning Natives, he found his way to Cibola, which is present day New Mexico. But there were no shining golden cities; the villages he found were ordinary, with dirt streets and adobe houses.

Still searching, convinced that the stories he'd heard must be true, he sent scouts out in different directions to search for the Cities of Gold. But instead, they found the Colorado River and, by following it, became the first Europeans to look upon one of nature's greatest spectacles: the Grand Canyon, almost 300 miles long, 18 miles wide, and more than a mile deep.

After the winter of 1541, Coronado and his men trekked onward, roving hundreds of miles through Texas. They saw herds of bison that seemed limitless and huge cities of teepees set up by the Native Americans who were following the beasts. Eventually, ranging farther still, they found themselves in Kansas, where de Soto and his men were also wandering.

Between them, Coronado and de Soto explored thousands of miles of the land that would one day become the United

States of America. Yet, to what end did it bring them? Their goal was gold and treasure, and they found little of that. Instead they reaped only destruction, for Coronado's expedition returned empty-handed, and, since he had funded it himself, he was bankrupt and disgraced. And, as for de Soto, he fell prey to a raging fever and died on the banks of the Mississippi River in May of 1542.

So, was it all for nothing—the death and suffering and the thousands of miles traveled? For these men it may have seemed that way, since they found only poverty and death. But when we look at them from our vantage point, here far in the future, we can see it a little more clearly.

The outcomes of those far-flung journeys were equally far-reaching. The Spaniards brought horses to North America, and for the Natives of the Great Plains that was an enormous gift, one that would change their entire way of life. But the Spaniards also brought their European diseases to the Natives, against which the native people had no defense and from which many of them would die. The foods that people ate would be forever changed: Potatoes and tomatoes from South America made their way to the Old World; sugarcane from Asia and coffee from Africa became important crops grown in the New World. Smoke from tobacco grown in North America would fill the taverns and coffeehouses of Europe; slaves sold by their captors in Africa would be forced to labor on Caribbean plantations. An exchange had begun between Europe and the Americas, an exchange of plants, animals, and people that would transform the entire world, and it all began with these bold Spaniards, following in the path that Christopher Columbus had forged.

Chapter 7

The Last Voyage of the *Discovery*

Henry Hudson

You might remember that this story started with cinnamon, nutmeg, and pepper: all of the spices that were found only in Asia and were so coveted by the nations of Europe. The New World, for all of its wonders, was nevertheless not Asia; and so—despite the promise of America's vast lands—Asia continued to beckon to European merchants and kings. The Silk Road remained closed to them, and they still wanted to find a shorter route to Asian shores.

Unfortunately, expeditions in search of such a route were expensive. All of the explorers that we've seen thus far—Columbus, Cabot, the conquistadors—required a wealthy patron to supply them with ships, men, and supplies. The only one who paid for his own expedition was Coronado, and, as you now know, he ended up in deep poverty. A king or prince could provide the money to send out explorers, but what about a simple merchant? He might have fine English wool or barrels of French wine, things that he could sell at great profit in India or China, but how was he to get it there? The journey around the tip of Africa was long, and that route was, in any case, controlled by Portugal, since it was originally discovered by Portuguese sailors. Merchants all over Europe desperately needed a different way. But how could one merchant, alone, pay for an expedition to find it?

The answer, of course, is that one merchant, all by himself, could not. So, instead, the merchants of Europe began to band together, pooling their money and resources in groups called *trading companies*. A trading company was a *corporation*—a group of many individual members who all shared the same purpose—in which all of the members were *shareholders*. Each of them invested some money into the company, and thus each of them would receive a share, or a portion of the company's profits. Shares of a company are also sometimes called *stocks*; this is why even today you might hear your parents or a news program talking about the *stock market* in New York City. That's a place where stocks—shares of large companies—are bought and sold and traded.

In the Netherlands, in the year 1602, the Dutch East India Company was formed by a group of merchants. Its purpose was to trade with India, where much of Europe's cotton cloth came from, and also to gain access to the East Indies, the islands where so many of the spices were grown. Today we know these islands as the nation of Indonesia.

The Dutch East India Company received a royal charter from the Dutch government giving it a *monopoly* over the spice trade in the Indies; only this company, and no other, was allowed to trade for spices with the islanders and sell them in the Netherlands. The charter also gave the company the right to organize and govern any colonies it might choose to establish in the Indies. With the charter in hand, the Company needed only to find a better way to get there.

Thus it was that in 1609 the Dutch East India Company hired an Englishman named Henry Hudson to find a passage to India.

The Company's idea was to search to the northeast. They wanted Hudson to sail from Amsterdam as far north as he could, past Denmark and Norway, up around the northern coast of Russia toward the east and into the *Arctic Circle*, which is that line of latitude that marks the area circling the North Pole. They hoped that by doing so, he could sail up and over the top of the world and come down to Asia on the other side.

Hudson agreed to do so, but he must have had his doubts. This wasn't, you see, the first time that Hudson had attempted to find the Northeast Passage to Asia. Sailing for an English trading company, he had pierced the Arctic Circle and attempted to sail past Russia two previous times, in 1607 and 1608, and both times had found the way blocked by impassible ice. It appears he had no reason to think that his attempt for the Dutch East India Company would produce a different result.

Henry Hudson departed from the Dutch capital of Amsterdam on April 4, 1609, accompanied by his young son John. They sailed in a Dutch ship christened *Half Moon*. By mid-May they were in the Arctic Ocean off the coast of Norway, but, as Hudson might have predicted, the way ahead was choked with huge rafts of gleaming blue ice. He gave the order to turn the ship about.

It was here, though, that Henry Hudson made a fateful decision. Instead of veering south and returning to Amsterdam, he ordered the ship to tack to the west and strike out across the Atlantic toward North America.

Hudson, you see, had been listening to rumors. A Venetian explorer named Giovanni da Verrazzano, following in the wake of John Cabot, had explored in 1524 a bay on the North American coast into which flowed a large river. Perhaps, the rumors suggested, this river or another like it might flow all the way through the North American continent. If a person could find such a river, he would be able to sail up the river directly west, passing all the way through the continent and out into the Pacific Ocean and then on to Asia. It would be the Northwest Passage, a shortcut to end all shortcuts! And then, just as Hudson was preparing to leave on this voyage, he received a letter and a package of maps from a friend, Captain John Smith, whom you will meet again in a chapter to come. Captain Smith mentioned that the Native Americans, too, spoke of large rivers leading off toward the west. Surely such possibilities must be explored! The Dutch East India Company had not authorized Hudson to make any changes in plans, but Hudson knew that, were he to find the Northwest Passage, he would return to Amsterdam in triumph, and all would be forgiven.

A two-month voyage across the North Atlantic brought them to the land called Nova Scotia in Canada. Slowly they made their way south until they came in September to the large bay that Verrazzano had described, a bay that we know today as New York Harbor. As rumored, a large river emptied into the bay, and, on September 11, the *Half Moon* set sail up this river.

But the summer was gone, and autumn was upon them. After 10 days, Hudson decided reluctantly that they must, for now, give up the search for the Northwest Passage and return to Europe. The *Half Moon* docked in Dartmouth, England, in early November, but, instead of a warm welcome, Hudson found himself in deep trouble. The English trading companies were furious that he, an Englishman, should have made this bold expedition in service of the Dutch! They locked him up and demanded that he hand over his ship's log and all the records of his voyage. But they were too late, for Hudson had managed to smuggle the log to the Dutch ambassador who lived in England, and he in turn had assured Hudson that it and all its information would be sent to the Dutch East India Company. Hudson was hustled off to a nearby house and forbidden to leave it; the king of England himself ordered that Hudson never again be allowed to explore on behalf of any other country.

But Hudson's dream of a northwest passage did not die. In 1610 he was allowed to set forth once more, this time aboard an English ship, the *Discovery*. His son John was again at his side, and hope filled their sails. After all, it seemed only logical that such a huge mass of land as North America would be carved with many rivers. Surely one of them led all the way through! It was just a matter of finding it.

This time, Hudson ventured farther to the north, to test how far he could go before polar ice blocked the way. He passed the enormous island of Greenland in June, and by the end of that month he was once again in sight of North America, reaching that part of far northeastern Canada that is now called Labrador. He maneuvered through a *strait*—a narrow strip of water between two land masses on each side—made perilous indeed by terrifyingly strong currents, and out into a massive body of water so large that the crew were convinced they had found the Pacific Ocean. When it became clear that this was instead an enormous bay, their enthusiasm did not fade: this must instead be the opening mouth of the Northwest Passage!

Eagerly they began to probe forward, mapping the edges of the bay, confident that soon they would reach the Pacific. But months slipped by, and no passage through was found. Supplies were running low, and the crew began to lose faith. Low, grumbling talk spread among the men, just as slow, creeping ice began to carpet the surface of the bay.

By November, retreat was impossible. The *Discovery* was trapped in the ice, and Hudson and his men had no choice but to make their way to shore and build a camp in which to spend a frigid, miserable winter.

When the ice finally cleared, late the next spring, Hudson's spirits lifted. Onward they would go! The Northwest Passage was within their grasp! But the crew had no such confidence. The men were weak and sick, many of them starving, and they wanted nothing more than to sail back through the strait, across the ocean, and home. When Hudson angrily refused to do this, the crew came to a dark decision: rather than follow Hudson on his continued quest, they would *mutiny*.

On the 23rd of June, 1611, the men of the crew seized Hudson, his son John, and seven other crew members, who had remained loyal to Hudson and were also very sick, and threw them all into a *shallop*, a smaller boat that had been attached to the *Discovery*. They pushed the shallop away, setting it adrift, and then unfurled the *Discovery*'s sails and glided off, leaving Hudson and the others to their fates there on the cold waters of the bay.

Henry Hudson was never seen again.

But he did not disappear, not entirely; for the river running into New York Harbor is called the Hudson River, and Hudson's explorations there gave the Dutch the confidence and authority to claim that area as the colony of New Netherland. The strait that the *Discovery* entered is now called the Hudson Strait, which became the gateway for many other expeditions engaged in a search for the elusive Northwest Passage to Asia. And the bay beyond, the enormous Hudson Bay, would become a center for a fur-trading empire that would change the fate of nations.

For Henry Hudson, the voyage of the *Discovery* brought a painful end. But New Netherland was just beginning, and with it a whole new dawn: the birth and growth of the American colonies.

Chapter 8

The Lost Colony

Roanoke

Sir Walter Raleigh

Sir Walter Raleigh had a problem. He was a dashing English gentleman: a poet, a soldier, a spy, an explorer, and, occasionally, a pirate. He was also a great favorite of the English queen, Elizabeth I, and her affection for him was the source of his problem. The queen, you see, had in the year 1584 granted a charter to Raleigh giving him the right to plant an English colony in the New World. But the charter specified that this colony must be fully established within six years. Time was pressing, and Raleigh needed to make a beginning; unfortunately, the queen had forbidden him to leave her side.

Queen Elizabeth I of England

Since he could not embark on the New World adventure himself, Raleigh was forced to assign the task of colony building to others. He chose two men, Philip Amadas and Arthur Barlowe, and sent them off, each in command of a ship. By July of 1584 the two vessels had landed at Roanoke Island, off the shore of what is now North Carolina. They were greeted by Native Americans who impressed the Englishmen with the peacefulness of their villages and the bounty of their crops. When the two men returned to England a few weeks later, they brought with them glowing tales of the suitability of that land for a colony along with two Native men named Wanchese and Manteo to give witness to the truth of these reports.

The queen was pleased. She declared that the island and all the mainland surrounding it should be called "Virginia," after her own nickname: The Virgin Queen. She praised Raleigh and dubbed him a knight as well as "Lord Protector and Governor of Virginia." Now, more than ever, Raleigh must make a success of his colony there.

Still tied to the queen's side, he once again sent others. Sir Richard Grenville, one of Her Majesty's naval commanders, led the mission as its admiral along with a man named Ralph Lane who would be the colony's governor. The expedition also included several scientists, an artist named John White, the Natives Wanchese and Manteo, and 100 Englishmen. They arrived in the Virginia territory in June of 1585 and, after surveying the area for a month or so, decided to place the colony on Roanoke Island, where Amadas and Barlowe had already formed good relations with the native people. Manteo offered to negotiate with the leader of the nearby tribe who in turn gave the Englishmen some land on which to settle on the north end of the island.

The men set about building a fort, although almost all of them were eager to explore, certain that heaping piles of gold and silver were out there somewhere just waiting to be scooped up. But Lane kept them busy with construction work, preferring instead to leave the exploring to one of the scientists, Thomas Harriot, and the artist John White, whom he sent out with one of the expedition's smaller boats. Lord Grenville, meanwhile, returned to England with his ship, promising to return in a few months with more colonists.

Harriot and White made their way from village to village, acquainting themselves with the native tribes and scouting the abundant resources that Virginia offered: fish, game, timber, even some copper. They found no piles of gold and silver and no immense cities such as the conquistadors had discovered among the Inca and the Aztec to the south. But the villages were secure and prosperous, and the Natives obviously well understood how to make a good living on the land.

As their journey continued, though, Harriot and White began to notice something strange: after they had visited a village, it would shortly be overtaken by sickness—a deadly influenza or the dreaded smallpox. Smallpox had been known in Europe and Asia for centuries where it had killed many people. In our modern times, this sickness has been completely vanquished. But the New World, in those days, had never seen this disease, and the people who lived there had no defense against it, nor did they understand that diseases are transmitted by viruses and germs. Although Harriot and White and the other Englishmen did not realize it and certainly did not intend it, they were spreading European diseases among the North American natives. The same sicknesses were spreading in South America, too, brought unwittingly by the conquistadors and their men, a tragic part of the great exchange between the Old World and the New.

When Harriot and White returned to the Roanoke colony, they found it struggling. Supplies were running short, and the Natives, who had initially been helpful, were growing weary of the Englishmen and their constant demands for more food. By the spring of 1586, the men of the colony were spiritless, half-starved, and desperate.

It was then that a fleet of English ships suddenly appeared just offshore, led by Sir Francis Drake, a bold explorer and sometime pirate who was returning to England after a successful expedition preying upon Spanish ships in the Caribbean Sea. When he saw the sad state of the Roanoke colony, he gave them food and tools and offered to leave them one of his ships, the *Francis*. But before they could take advantage of his offer, a fierce storm struck the island. The *Francis* was blown out to sea and sunk, and, with this loss, the men of the colony lost all heart as well. They asked Drake to take them all back to England.

Two weeks later, a fleet of ships captained by Lord Grenville lowered their anchors at Roanoke, stuffed to the rails with supplies and 100 new colonists. Grenville scoured the island, searching for the men who should have been there, little knowing that they'd all just abandoned the colony and sailed off with Sir Francis Drake. Finally, they found a Native man who was willing to tell them what had happened. Grenville, no doubt with a sigh of frustration, left 15 men behind to make certain that Raleigh's claim to Virginia remained intact. He gave them enough supplies for two years and turned back toward England. We can only imagine what those men must have felt as they watched the ships' sails disappear over the eastern horizon.

Upon their return to England, Thomas Harriot and John White sought out Sir Walter Raleigh and persuaded him to make one last attempt. Naming John White as governor, Raleigh organized another expedition, this one fully focused on founding a real town with women and children, farmers and craftsmen. Among the 115 colonists who volunteered were John White's daughter, Eleanor, and her husband, Ananias Dare.

They arrived at Roanoke Island on July 22, 1587, and were met with an ominous silence. The fort was destroyed, and there was no sign of the 15 men who'd been left behind by Grenville. An uneasy report reached them through Manteo that the men had all been killed. Just a day or so later, one of their own shipmates was struck down by Native arrows as he was searching the deserted beach for crabs to eat.

Manteo tried to smooth out relations between the colonists and the nearby Native tribes, but neither group trusted the other, and grim forebodings shadowed them. Nevertheless, the colony rejoiced just a few weeks later when Eleanor Dare gave birth to a baby girl, the first English child born in North America. Her parents named her Virginia.

Summer was passing quickly. The colonists planted crops and built homes. There were no more hostilities with the Natives, but the colonists knew that their situation was dire. They did not have enough food, weapons, ammunition, and tools to sustain themselves. They persuaded their governor, John White, to return to England with the ships that had brought them and come back to them the next spring with the needed supplies. Reluctantly, he agreed, but only if the colonists would promise that, if they ran into trouble, they would carve a distinctive cross on a tree near the fort. Then he kissed his daughter and his new granddaughter goodbye.

He arrived back in England in November of that year only to discover, to his horror, that England was at war with Spain. Queen Elizabeth wanted every single English ship to protect the English coast. Despite John White's desperate pleas and his tale of the suffering that the colonists on Roanoke Island would surely endure, there was no ship to take either him or any supplies back across the Atlantic.

Only when the war ended, three years later, was John White able to hire some ships. How frantic he must have felt! Three long years, during which he could receive no word from his daughter and her family. Three long years, during which his imagination must have continually assailed him with all the dangers and disasters that the colony would face. It might give us pause to learn that one of the ships that John White was finally able to secure for his rescue mission was named the *Hopewell*. Indeed, hope was really all that he had.

The *Hopewell* sighted Roanoke Island on the evening of August 17, 1590. The sailors spied at once a bonfire burning on the north end of the island. How John White's heart must have leapt! Someone at least was still alive! But it was too dark to row ashore, and so he must wait, surely consumed with impatience, for the next day, August 18, which was little Virginia Dare's third birthday.

The next morning, the *Hopewell* sent a boat ashore with John White and several others. Eagerly they raced to the site of the colony, but they found . . . no one. The colony wasn't destroyed. The houses weren't burnt or fallen down; there were no signs of a panicked withdrawal. But eerie silence blanketed the town, and not one person could be discovered. John White and the men scoured the whole area, looking for any clue, searching especially for the carved cross which would signal that the colonists had been in distress. But, instead, they found something strange.

On a nearby tree, carved in stark, block letters, there was one word: CROATOAN.

John White must have felt hope take root once more—for one of the islands nearby was named Croatoan Island; surely this brief message meant that the colonists had moved there. But before the *Hopewell* and its sister ships could investigate, terrible, stormy weather descended upon them. The *Hopewell's* anchor cable snapped, and the fierce waves put the little fleet in grave danger. Reluctantly, they turned sail, back toward England.

John White was heartbroken. Though he never gave up hope, he knew that he must surrender his family "to the merciful help of the Almighty, whom I most humbly beseech to help and comfort them."

Others would search for the colony, including Walter Raleigh himself, but the colonists of Roanoke were never found. No trace of them was discovered on Croatoan Island or, indeed, anywhere else. Were they killed by hostile Natives? Perhaps. Did they give up the terrible struggle of building their own town and go to live among the neighboring tribes? Perhaps. In the years to come, other colonists and explorers would continue to hear reports of light-haired and gray-eyed Natives, descendants perhaps of Roanoke's people. But no one can say for certain. The Lost Colony of Roanoke remains one of America's great mysteries.

Chapter 9

Work to Eat

The Adventurers of Jamestown

When England's Queen Elizabeth I died in 1603, there were no English settlers in North America. Roanoke had been a noble failure. Elizabeth's throne was assumed by her cousin, James VI of Scotland, who became King James I of England. By 1604, he had made peace with Spain and could turn his attention once more to the New World. He had seen the gold that the Spaniards were taking out of South America and the huge profits they were making from their Caribbean sugar plantations. He did not want England to be left behind.

So he created the Virginia Company, a trading company much like the Dutch East India Company. It had a single mission: to harvest the resources of North America—gold, furs, timber, fish. The only way to do that was to build a permanent colony.

You might be wondering about that word: *colony*. What exactly does it mean? A colony is an area in one land that is controlled by people from another land. For example, you might have a nice backyard, perhaps with a stone-paved patio. Suppose you wake up one morning to discover that your neighbor has moved several deck chairs, a hammock stand, and a barbecue grill onto your patio. You didn't ask him to do this, and he didn't necessarily ask for permission. He has just moved in and taken over that portion of your backyard. He has colonized your patio.

Of course, he could also move his deck chairs into the empty lot across the street or into the middle of the forest outside of town. But, wherever he makes his new patio, he is exercising control and ownership over land that is outside the boundaries of his own land. That's what makes it a colony.

"All right," you might say, "That makes sense, but what if that land already belongs to someone else? Isn't that stealing?" And the answer is yes, of course, it certainly is. When the Spaniards, following in the wake of Columbus, swept through the Aztec and Inca empires of South America, they were not merely moving in. They came to conquer.

But, in North America, it was a bit different. We have seen, of course, that many Natives lived in North America, but they were spread out over the vast expanse of the continent. The northeastern coast—where explorers such as Verrazzano or Cabot had landed—seemed to them rather sparsely occupied. Explorers found Native American villages, but they saw no giant cities or great empires such as those governed by the Aztec or the Inca. The land seemed so broad, with so much room. Thus, at least at first, the settlers who came planned to live alongside the Native people peacefully. You will remember, from the last chapter, that the Native Manteo sought and was given permission by the local chief for the Roanoke settlers to build their fort on the north end of the island. This is not to say that all the Englishmen who would come to the New World viewed the Natives with compassion or respect. Some did, certainly, but others saw them only as frightful savages. The conflict between those two viewpoints would sadly lead to much trouble and bloodshed in the future.

In any case, when he created the Virginia Company, King James authorized the men who were putting money into it—its *investors*—to establish a colony somewhere along the shores of

Virginia. So it was that, in May of 1607, after four stormy months tossed upon the sea, three tiny ships loaded with 109 men and boys ventured into Chesapeake Bay.

Chesapeake Bay is a wonder; it is America's largest *estuary*— that is, a place where the ocean reaches inland to shake hands with a freshwater river. If you look at a map of the United States and search for the states of Virginia and Maryland, you will see Chesapeake Bay wedged between them like the strong, twisted root of a mighty tree.

The three ships—the *Susan Constant,* the *Discovery,* and the *Godspeed*—were all under the authority of Captain Christopher Newport. He found a river near the south end of the bay that seemed promising; it had a northwestern bend to it, and, like all of those who'd come before, these colonists were hopeful of finding a river route through the continent to Asia: the Northwest Passage. The colonists christened this river the James River in honor of the English king. Over the next few weeks, they made their way up the river until they came to a large peninsula about 40 miles inland. It seemed like a good place: deserted and easily defensible. Departing their ships, they set about constructing a fort along with some thatched-roof huts for houses and a church. They called their new home Jamestown.

Their first task was planting crops, for they desperately needed food in order to survive. Unfortunately, though, most of these would-be colonists were townsmen and gentlemen adventurers unaccustomed to the labor of farming. Almost all of them had come to find gold; they hadn't expected to spend their days breaking ground and toiling over the land. They didn't understand the rhythms and patterns of the wildlife, either, and so did not know how to fish or hunt. Fresh supplies from England could not be counted on, and, indeed, a successful colony must be able to support itself, which these men did not seem prepared to work for. Jamestown might have failed utterly, another Roanoke, except for the efforts and talents of one man: Captain John Smith.

John Smith, too, was an adventurer. His whole life had been spent seeking his own fortune, for his father had died when John was young, and he'd had no choice but to rely on his own devices. He'd been a merchant, a sailor, and a *mercenary*—a soldier who hires himself out to fight for pay. He'd fought duels, been sold into slavery and escaped it, and traveled all over Europe by foot and on horseback. In 1606 he joined the Virginia Company and set sail with the expedition.

One of the original buildings of the settlement at Jamestown

His voyage to the New World was anything but pleasant. He argued heatedly with Christopher Newport who grew so enraged that he charged Smith with mutiny and imprisoned him in a cell below deck. He planned to execute Smith as soon as the ships landed in Virginia, but that was not to be. When land was reached, Newport's first responsibility was to open a packet of sealed orders sent by the investors of the Virginia Company. When he did so, he discovered to his great chagrin that John Smith had been appointed one of the new colony's governors.

Newport had no choice but to set Smith free, and so John Smith found himself at Jamestown, watching things go awry.

And go awry they did. The colonists had been pleased to find a site unoccupied by Native tribes, but now they realized that this was because the place they had chosen was swampy and plagued by mosquitoes. The stores of food they had brought from England were running so low that each man was given just one cup of grain to eat each day. By September, only a few months after they had landed, 60 men had died. Still, the colonists were heedless. During that winter, they set Jamestown on fire through sheer carelessness and were then forced to shelter from the cold in the smoke-blackened ruins. When spring came and Captain Newport returned from England, they used the precious time when the ship was anchored there not to rebuild or to plant crops, but instead to load its hull to the brim with many, many pounds of a shiny rock that they'd found near the riverbed. Though they were certain it was gold, it was actually a worthless mineral called iron pyrite, which even now we call "fool's gold." They continued to die from starvation and disease.

But John Smith was not the sort of man to stand by and let things fall apart. He knew that the colonists needed to better understand this land if they were to survive. He began to explore, surveying Chesapeake Bay and creating a map of Virginia that would be used by New World colonists for the next hundred years.

Late in 1607, as he was far from Jamestown scouting the countryside, Smith was set upon by a hunting party of Native Americans who, after a pitched battle, captured him. These were a people called the Powhatan. Their leader, though his name was Wahunsunacock, was also called Powhatan, and he ruled over a collection of some 30 or so tribes. He was wary of these English newcomers, even though he understood that they might be useful allies for trade and military strength against his enemies. Legend tells us that when John Smith was brought before him that day, Powhatan decided to have him killed. At the last moment, though, his young daughter, Pocahontas, interceded. She ran forward, cradled Smith's head in her arms, and persuaded her father to set him free.

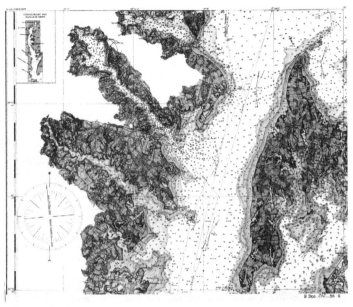

Chesapeake Bay

After this rescue, John Smith took leadership over the Jamestown colony. At once he instituted a new rule: "If a man will not work, he shall not eat." No more aimless searching for gold, no more lazing about the ruins of the fort. He insisted that every man in the colony do a day's work in order to receive a day's food. He also bargained with Powhatan for corn and learned from the Natives better ways to farm and fish. For most of that year, Pocahontas herself would visit Jamestown every week or so, bringing corn and other provisions and joining the younger boys in their games.

These fruitful efforts and friendly relations might have paved the way for a stronger Jamestown, but in 1609 John

Smith met with a terrible accident. While paddling alone in a canoe, the gunpowder that he was carrying exploded, and he was badly burned. He was forced to return to England when the next supply ship came and went.

Statue of Pocahontas at Historic Jamestown

With John Smith gone, so too departed his strong leadership. The colony's disciplined ways evaporated like a mist, and disorder once again ruled the day. During the winter of 1609 through 1610, the colony suffered intensely, so much so that they called it "The Starving Time." When another supply ship arrived the next spring, only 60 men in the colony were still alive. Desperate to keep their investment afloat, the Virginia Company sent yet another shipload of colonists.

Among them was John Rolfe who carried with him a packet of tobacco seeds. Tobacco, you might know, is a plant whose leaves can be crushed into a pipe or rolled into a cylinder and smoked. Soon, Rolfe was harvesting tobacco and shipping it off to England where it sold for a tremendous profit. During this time, he met and married Pocahontas, cementing, for a few years at least, a peace between Jamestown and the Powhatan people. Sadly, though, Pocahontas became sick during a trip with her husband to England and died there on March 21, 1617. The following year, her father also died. As the English continued to take more land to plant tobacco fields, the friendship between the Powhatan people and the English colonists faded into suspicion and mistrust.

Meanwhile, back in England, recovering from his injuries, John Smith was writing. In his letters and books, he urged his fellow Englishmen to become colonists. The land, he wrote, was overflowing with good things. Much prosperity could come to any man who would go there, as long as he was willing to work hard. Go west, he said. Go to the New World, and let it fill you up.

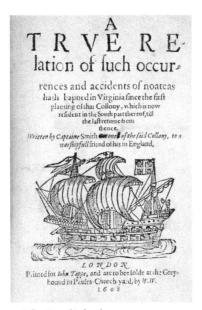

Page from Captain John Smith's book

Chapter 10

Across the Vast and Furious Ocean
The Mayflower

On November 11, 1620, the good ship *Mayflower* lay at anchor in a large natural harbor north of Virginia, a place that Captain John Smith had mapped and given a name: Cape Cod.

The little ship was full to bursting with passengers, mostly men—some of them farmers and craftsmen, some of them soldiers, some alone, and some with their wives and children in tow. They had been voyaging for more than two months through rough seas, and many of them were sick or injured. Nevertheless, on that morning, in the middle of November, 41 of them gathered in the *Mayflower's* belly. On a sea-chest in their midst lay a sheet of parchment on which had been scratched a few sentences. One by one each of the 41 men bent over it and, with a quill dipped in rusty black ink, signed his name.

By signing, each was pledging his agreement to the truths that were laid out there: that they were all servants of God and loyal subjects to the King of England; that they had journeyed across the ocean to plant a new colony; that the colony must have laws and government in order to avoid chaos and destruction; and that laws and government would only work if each man promised to help create them and then obey them. The parchment and the words it contained would bind them together into a "Civil Body Politick": a group working together as one to govern themselves.

The Mayflower Compact

The paper they signed is called today the Mayflower Compact. A handwritten copy is still kept safely preserved in the State Library of Massachusetts.

Like the settlers at Jamestown, the passengers of the *Mayflower* were Englishmen, given permission by the Virginia Company to form a colony in the New World. But there the resemblance ended. For unlike the adventurers of Jamestown, many of these colonists were driven not by dreams of gold or the lure of discovery; their greatest desire was to worship God freely in the way that seemed right to them and to live together in quiet peace. In order to achieve that goal, they had journeyed many, many weary miles, and so we call them Pilgrims: travelers with a sacred end in sight.

Originally, they had lived in the small village of Scrooby, right in the center of England. In those days, the king of

England had decreed that every English person must go to church every Sunday, rain or shine, and, furthermore, he or she must attend the official Church of England, created by King Henry VIII nearly 90 years earlier in 1534. But there were many who believed that the Church of England had strayed from the true path, that it was corrupt and even ungodly, and, most of all, that the king had no right to interfere in any single Christian's practice of his faith. Those who thought this way were called Dissenters and Separatists, because they *dissented,* or disagreed, with the Church of England, and because they believed that true Christians must separate from it. The people in the little church in Scrooby were Separatists.

As time went by, as they persisted in their beliefs, more and more trouble came to them. They were forced to pay fines for not attending the king's church; they were viewed with suspicion and distrust by their neighbors. And then, in 1607, the leader of the Church of England ordered that their homes in Scrooby be invaded by soldiers and the leaders of their church put in prison. Frightened and shaken, they decided that they must leave England entirely in order to escape the persecution being heaped upon them.

At first, under the guidance of their leader, William Brewster, they determined to go to the Netherlands, where there was no decree from any king to prevent them from worshiping God however they liked. But now a different sort of trouble plagued them: Holland was a foreign place, with customs and language and expectations wholly unlike their home back in Scrooby. It was hard for the men to find jobs to support their families, and, to their dismay, they found their children becoming less and less English and more and more like the Dutch. Then, in 1618, English soldiers came to Holland with orders to arrest William Brewster and haul him back to England in chains, there to answer for his continued criticism of the Church of England. He managed to escape arrest, but it was clear to all of them that they were still in grave danger. The Netherlands was no longer a haven for them; in fact, they felt they needed to leave Europe entirely.

And so, in 1619, they obtained permission from the Virginia Company to sail to the New World and found a colony at the mouth of the Hudson River. A group of investors called the Merchant Adventurers lent them the money to buy two ships, the *Speedwell* and the *Mayflower*, and stock them with supplies. In July of 1620, after months of delay spent gathering needed provisions and wrangling with the Merchant Adventurers about exactly how much money they owed, the Pilgrims boarded the *Speedwell* at a dock in the Netherlands and set sail for the west coast of England where they would meet up with the *Mayflower* and William Brewster who had been in hiding all these months since the soldiers had tried to arrest him in Holland.

Before they could set sail, they were joined by a group of men that they called "the Strangers": soldiers, craftsmen, adventurers, and servants who had been recruited by the Merchant Adventurers to help set up the colony. Among them was the colony's new military expert, a soldier named Captain Myles Standish. The Pilgrims accepted these companions reluctantly, recognizing their need for help but knowing, also, that these strangers did not share the strong beliefs that had sent the Pilgrims on this journey. On August 5, 1620, the two ships left England with about 120 passengers—Pilgrims and Strangers alike.

But trouble still followed them. The *Speedwell* began to leak, slowly at first and then so badly that the group had no choice but to turn around and return to the English port of Plymouth. Repairs proved impossible, and, in despair, some of the party abandoned the expedition entirely. But many wished to press on, and that meant that they must squeeze aboard the already desperately crowded *Mayflower*. Every day they spent in port meant more money wasted in lost provisions and port fees and more money owed to the Merchant Adventurers; worse still, it was getting later and later in the year, and leaving now meant arriving in the New World just as the winter winds were starting to howl. But what choice did they have? With the Pilgrims' prayers directed heavenward and undoubtedly some grumbling and muttering among the Strangers, the *Mayflower* set out across the Atlantic on September 6 with 102 passengers and 30 crewmen on board.

The next two months were bitter. Strong gales shook the ship as it crept forward, bending and stretching it so severely that it sprang leaks all across its length, and the main beam that supported the ship's frame cracked. Almost every person on board suffered from dreadful bouts of seasickness; one of the Pilgrims died, and another, Susanna White, grew ever more heavily pregnant and began to fear that she would be forced to give birth to her baby on board the crowded, heaving ship. And, when they finally sighted land in early November, the shallow, dangerous coastline and swirling tides prevented them from sailing south to find their landing site, the mouth of the Hudson River.

Exhausted and hungry, with winter on the near horizon, they decided to take shelter in the safest place they could find, the harbor of Cape Cod Bay. There they dropped their anchor on November 11.

But the trading company had not given them permission to settle anywhere but the Hudson River, and the Strangers objected strongly: the colony would have no legal right to exist anywhere else. A Pilgrim leader named William Bradford later wrote that several of the Strangers "made discontented and mutinous speeches." To calm their spirits and to bring the whole group together, the Pilgrims drafted the Mayflower Compact, making it clear that the colony would be governed by "just and equal laws" for everyone who would live there. With that established, both Strangers and Pilgrims were satisfied and ready to begin the great work of building a home in the New World. That same week, aboard the Mayflower, Susanna White gave birth to a baby boy, Peregrine White, the first child born to the Pilgrims in America.

Their first task was to find a suitable site for their new town. With Captain Myles Standish at its head, a group of men went out to explore. Sleet, fog, snow, and cold winter rain discouraged them, and they found no place that would seem to fulfill all their requirements: a site easy to guard and defend; plenty of flat, clear ground for growing crops; and clean, sweet water. Then, on December 8, they encountered some Native Americans, and the meeting went quickly sour, with gunshots fired and hostility on both sides. Discouraged and fearing that they had angered their potential Native neighbors by firing at them, the Pilgrims decided to pull up the anchor and sail on a bit further.

By December 16, they had found another bay, an offshoot of the larger Cape Cod Bay, with a gentle harbor protected by a long beach to the south and another to the north. For the next three days, the men searched for a good place to build, deciding at last upon the site of an abandoned Native American village perched above the harbor on two rounded hills. The hills were easily defended, the land was already cleared for farming, and fresh water flowed nearby. With thankful hearts, the Pilgrims named it Plymouth, after the last port they'd left in England so many weeks before.

William Bradford, writing later, described how they felt:

"Being thus arrived in a good harbor, and brought safe to land, they fell upon their knees and blessed the God of Heaven, who had brought them over the vast and furious ocean, and delivered them from all the perils and miseries thereof, again to set their feet on the firm and stable earth, their proper element."

They had survived the troubles that had beset them. There might be more to come, of course, but here, just before Christmas in the year 1620, the Pilgrims had finally reached their true home.

Chapter 11

New Amsterdam, New France, and New England

The Old World Claims the New World

When Henry Hudson brought news to the Dutch of the rolling river that now bears his name and the deep harbor into which it empties, he saw fit to mention something else: that the land along the river, and far to the north as well, was home to a creature that might prove valuable to the Dutch traders and merchantmen. This was the beaver; its fur was greatly desired in Europe for the making of soft, luxurious, waterproof hats.

The Dutch wasted no time. They could see that the mouth of the Hudson River provided an ideal spot to establish a trading center for all the riches that could be harvested from the New World. By 1621, just as the Pilgrims were settling in at Plymouth Colony, the Dutch had created a new trading company—the Dutch West India Company—and had made friendly agreements with the Native people, offering to buy beaver pelts from Native hunters. The Company then found 30 families who were willing to make the voyage to the New World. They arrived in 1624, charged with the task of setting up a fortress on the southern tip of an island at the Hudson River's mouth, an island named Manhattan.

The Native Americans who lived there called it Manah-ahtaan, which means "the place for gathering wood to make bows." By 1626, though, the leaders of the Dutch colonists had met with them and offered to buy the land. In a letter to the Dutch king, an officer of the Dutch West India Company reported that "our people are in good spirit and live in peace. The women also have borne some children there. They have purchased the Island Manhattes from the Indians for the value of 60 guilders." Sixty guilders, in those days, was enough money to buy a pound and a half of silver.

Slowly, the settlers began to establish a life on the island. They constructed a fort, which eventually contained a church, quarters for the soldiers who manned the fort, a house for the Director of the Dutch West India Company, and a warehouse for the beaver pelts that were bound for Europe and its hat makers. They built houses on the land surrounding the fort and then a wall to protect the new little town. An old Native American trail led away from the fort; the settlers widened it, naming it Broadway, while the road that ran along the wall itself became Wall Street. By 1645, there were more than a thousand souls living there along the Hudson River. Their settlement was a real town now, called New Amsterdam after the great Dutch capital city. The vast region that surrounded it was named New Netherland. Like the English and the Spanish before them, the Dutch had planted their feet firmly in the New World.

At the same time, farther north, the French were seeking to do the same. For France, though, the lure of North America had little to do with setting up colonies. They were drawn by the still bright hope of finding the Northwest Passage to Asia and by the quick wealth to be gained from beaver pelts.

France's first expedition to the New World had been captained by Giovanni de Verrazzano who, as you might remember, explored the northeastern coast of the continent in the 1520s and first set eyes on the lovely bay that would one day be called New York Harbor.

After him came Jacques Cartier in 1534. He ventured even farther to the north than Verrazzano and found another great inlet of water. Because he entered it on the feast day of St. Lawrence, a church holiday, he named it the Gulf of St. Lawrence, and the river that flowed into it, the St. Lawrence River. The Native people he met there directed him to a nearby *kanata*, which was their word for "village." With this conversation in mind, Cartier named the land on both sides of the St. Lawrence River "the Country of Canadas," which of course would one day become the nation of Canada. In 1541, Cartier led a group of settlers up the St. Lawrence river, hoping to build a permanent town and to keep searching for a route to Asia. But the winter was harsh; the Natives who lived there, the Iroquois, were suspicious of these newcomers; the Northwest Passage continued to be elusive; and the efforts to build floundered. Instead, the would-be settlers spent their time digging up the gleaming crystals and nuggets of shining rock that littered the ground, certain that they had found a *motherlode* of diamonds and gold. When Cartier returned to France with a ship full of this bounty, however, it was discovered to be merely crystals of quartz and iron pyrite, the rock that we call "fool's gold," which, you might remember, had also deceived the adventurers at Jamestown. Faced with this disappointment, many in France concluded that the New World had little to offer.

But other Frenchmen disagreed, pointing to the thick, soft beaver pelts and the many friendly Natives who were willing to trade them in return for European-made tools and cloth. One who believed strongly in the possibilities of this fur trade was Samuel de Champlain who arrived from France in 1608 and sailed up the St. Lawrence River. He wrote, "I arrived there on the 3rd of July, when I searched for a place suitable for our settlement; but I could find none more convenient or better suited than the point of Quebec, so called by the [Natives], which was covered with nut-trees." Champlain succeeded where Cartier had not: the settlement of Quebec grew and flourished. Today it is one of North America's greatest cities; in 1608, it was the birthplace of New France.

From this beginning on the St. Lawrence River, Champlain set about establishing the French fur trade. He made *alliances*— agreements to live and trade in peace—with the nearby Native tribes, the Algonquin and the Huron, and supported them in their wars with the fierce Iroquois. He paid fair prices for furs that the Natives brought to him, but he also sent his own men out to live among them in their villages to learn their ways and, of course, to hunt for beaver. These young men were called *coureurs des bois,* which in the French language means "runners of the woods." They wandered far afield, sometimes remaining with their Native hosts for years at a time, and they spread the fur trade all along the shores of Hudson Bay and west to the Great Lakes and beyond. The citizens of New France were few, and they were scattered widely, but they were learning about the country and its native inhabitants, and their trading networks grew powerful and exceedingly profitable.

Far from Hudson Bay, the Pilgrims in Plymouth were not concerned with profit. Their eyes remained focused on God, and their desire was to see their little colony blossom into a heaven on earth where Christian people would live together in simplicity and holiness. But, at least at first, their lives in the New World were cruelly hard. After they landed in December of 1620, winter was looming over them, and in the months that followed, nearly half of them died of sickness and hunger. They might all have perished if it were not for help from an unexpected source: one day in March a Native American man walked boldly into the settlement and announced, "Welcome, Englishmen!"

His name was Samoset. In the days to come, he would introduce them to another Native, Squanto, who could speak their language, for he had been kidnapped in 1614 by an English sea captain and had spent several years in England. When he had finally returned to his home, he had found the villages deserted and all of his people gone. They had all died from the sicknesses brought by earlier European explorers, leaving only Squanto as the last of his tribe. But, sorrowful though that was, Squanto bore no ill will toward the Pilgrims. As that first spring melted into summer, he showed them how to grow corn, how to fish, how to hunt, and how to live well on the land. By fall, Plymouth was prospering with barns and sheds filled with the fruits of a bountiful harvest and a shipload of furs and timber to send back to England in payment of their debts to the Merchant Adventurers. They had also befriended the Wampanoags, the Native tribe who had adopted Squanto after the death of his own people. Together, Wampanoags and Pilgrims celebrated a harvest feast that we still enjoy today: Thanksgiving.

Jamestown and Plymouth were the first English colonies in North America, but others soon followed. In 1630, 11 ships bearing a group of 700 men, women, and children arrived in Massachusetts with a charter from the king granting them the land north of Plymouth. They, too, were following a divine mission. Like the Separatist Pilgrims, they believed that the Church in England was corrupt, but, instead of leaving it, they sought to purify it, to make it clean and holy. Because of this, they were called *Puritans*. Under the leadership of a Christian lawyer named John Winthrop, they wished to be a "city on a hill" whose light would beckon others to live in godly harmony. By the end of that year, another six or seven ships had landed with a thousand more colonists. At first, these Puritans called the city that they were building "Trimountaine" after the three hills upon which it sat, but its name was soon changed to the one it still bears: Boston.

Boston became the chosen destination for English settlers as more and more of them made their way to the New World. And, of course, conflicts arose as they often do among people, even those who are devoted to God. A young man named Roger Williams arrived in 1631, determined to live out his conviction that the king and government had no authority over the church. This was a belief that many of his new neighbors would have shared, but Roger Williams soon began to clash with the leaders in Boston over ideas like the proper treatment of their Native neighbors and the rules that governed church worship. His objections grew so forceful that, in 1635, he was banished from the Massachusetts colony and ordered to return to England. Instead, with a small group of followers, he moved south and purchased land from the Natives to build the town of Providence in a new colony that was called Rhode Island. That same year, another group of Puritans, led by a man named Thomas Hooker, ventured westward from Massachusetts and founded the colony of Connecticut. Neither of these new colonies possessed a charter from the king, but they followed the example of the Pilgrims with their Mayflower Compact and agreed together to govern themselves as they saw fit.

While all of this was happening, in the northern part of Virginia, yet another colony was born. In 1632, England's king, Charles I, granted a charter to an English nobleman named George Calvert, Lord Baltimore. Like the Puritans in Massachusetts and Roger Williams in Rhode Island, he was seeking a refuge for believers, although, in Calvert's case, the believers were English Catholics. Since the leader of their faith was the Pope in Rome rather than the Church of England, they faced violence and scorn. Calvert hoped to make a Catholic haven in his new colony, which was named Maryland in honor of the king's Catholic wife, Mary.

By the middle of the 1600s, then, the Old World of Europe had established its first outposts in the New World: New Netherland, with its fur-filled warehouses; New France, with its traders ranging far and wide; and New England, with its churches of the faithful. For now, they were isolated and separated, alone in the wilderness, but not for much longer. The New World had opened its doors, and many others were coming.

Chapter 12

The Gifts of Charles II

More English Colonies in America

Meanwhile, back in England, extraordinary things were happening.

After King James died in 1625, the English crown passed to his son, King Charles I. Like his father before him, Charles believed in the idea of "the divine right of kings": God had chosen the king, and the king sat on the throne in God's name, and therefore no one on earth could disobey or challenge the king's authority, even the English *Parliament*—the body of men who were England's lawmakers. The members of the Parliament disagreed and insisted that the king could not rule without Parliament's consent. This argument grew steadily more violent and spread to every corner of England. By 1642 the supporters of the king—the Royalists—were at war with the supporters of Parliament, who were called Roundheads. This was the English Civil War; a *civil war* is a conflict that is fought between citizens of the same country, brother against brother.

The leader of the Roundheads was a man named Oliver Cromwell, who was a Puritan. As we have seen, some of their fellow believers had journeyed afar to settle in the New World, but many Puritans still lived in England. Now they found themselves at odds with the King, fighting bloody battles to preserve their fervent belief in freedom to serve God as they saw fit. Because the King insisted that all of England's people continue to pray and worship only in the Church of England, the Roundheads, under Cromwell's leadership, fiercely opposed him. By 1649, the Roundheads had captured the king, put him on trial for the treasonous crime of making war on Parliament, and condemned him. Charles I was executed; his son, Charles II, fled the country, narrowly escaping capture himself. A new government, called the Commonwealth of England, was put into place with Oliver Cromwell as its ruler, the Lord Protector.

For the next nine years, Cromwell reigned in England, and Charles II languished in exile, spending those years in France and the Netherlands. When Cromwell died in 1658, his son Richard became Lord Protector, but he proved to be a weak and ineffective leader. England's Parliament, after wavering for a year or two, declared that Charles II had been the rightful king from the moment of his father's execution. They invited him to come back to England. Charles II made a triumphal return to London on May 29, 1660, his thirtieth birthday. On that day, he mounted his father's throne, an event that historians call the *Restoration* of the English monarchy.

All of this caused a great deal of interest and discussion and even unrest among England's American colonists. For, although they were focused on their own concerns—building farms, founding towns, and creating lives in their grand New World—they still thought of themselves as Englishmen, and the grievous war that was tearing England apart inflicted wounds on her colonies as well, with some people remaining loyal to the King and others staunchly Puritan, supporting Cromwell's Roundheads. But still, no matter where their sympathies lay, they could hardly have expected the offshoots that would blossom in the colonies from the seeds sown in the English Civil War.

You see, Charles II had been restored to a throne that wobbled unsteadily. His father had been defeated, dethroned, and executed; Charles had spent long years in exile and owed a great deal to those who had sheltered him and to family and friends who had worked, sometimes risking their own lives, to bring him back to the throne. He needed to strengthen his own power and to repay his debts. His gaze fell then on the New World with its tall forests and beaver-filled rivers, with its blooming tobacco fields and its ever-beckoning promise of gold. He decided to increase England's foothold in North America, rewarding his loyal friends by giving them vast territories there. The rich resources of the New World would multiply the gold in England's treasuries, and Charles's throne would be all the more secure.

So, in 1663, he granted eight noblemen, all of whom had assisted in his Restoration, a huge swath of land in the colony of Virginia, south of Jamestown. These friends of the king were eager to try their fortunes in the New World. Charles was just as eager to have them there, for by building towns and farms in Virginia, they would stand in the way of any northward expansion by the Spaniards down in Florida. He named the eight men *proprietors*, or owners, and they in turn called their colony Carolina, after the Latin form of Charles's name, *Carolus*.

Soon thereafter, Carolina boasted a bustling settlement: Charles Town—which would one day become the city of Charleston—surrounded by farms and cattle ranches. The Carolina soil was rich and deep, and the colony harvested bountiful crops of tobacco, rice, and indigo, a plant that produces a beautiful, vivid blue dye. In the northern half of the new colony, settlers gathered the sap from pine trees and boiled it down to make *turpentine,* a tar which was used to waterproof wooden ships. They would come to be called "Tar Heels," a nickname that would stick with the citizens of North Carolina right up into modern times.

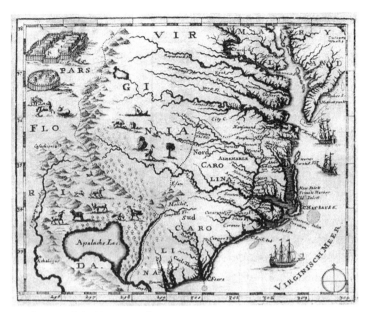

Early map of the Virginia colony

Meanwhile, King Charles, still giving gifts, was generously offering up land that was not necessarily his to give. He granted all of the land that the Dutch had claimed as New Netherland to his brother James, the Duke of York. After all, Charles argued, it was an English explorer, John Cabot, who had originally sailed along that coastline back in 1498, and so the land should be England's by right of first discovery. The Dutch, of course, disagreed entirely.

Thus it was that on August 27, 1664, at the Duke of York's command, four English warships sailed into New Amsterdam's harbor and sent a letter into the city demanding immediate surrender. It promised the Dutch settlers freedom and the right to keep their property as long as they would submit to the authority of the Duke of York and his brother the English king. But when this letter was brought to the Dutch governor of the island, Peter Stuyvesant, he sputtered with rage and tore it to shreds. He was a fierce, stubborn man, who had lost his leg to a cannonball and now stalked about proudly upon a stout wooden peg leg. He vowed to fight and sent messengers through the city to rouse the citizens of New Amsterdam. But they flatly refused him, unwilling to risk life or limb in a battle with the English; and so, having no soldiers, he was forced to accept the terms of surrender. The English took control of New Amsterdam and from there the entire colony of New Netherland, which they renamed New York in honor of James, the Duke of York. James himself would eventually become King of England in 1685, making New York a royal colony.

Following King Charles's example, in late 1664 the Duke of York gave a portion of New York to two of his friends as a repayment of debts that he owed to them. These men, John Berkeley and George Carteret, named their new colony New Jersey in honor of the Isle of Jersey off the coast of England, which was Carteret's ancestral home and whose people had always been steadfastly loyal to the king.

As the years of his reign stretched onward, Charles kept a close eye on the colonies. He wanted them to be stable and strong, to continue to grow and prosper. He recognized, for example, that the colonies of Rhode Island and Connecticut did not have any genuine legal right to govern themselves, since neither of them possessed a charter. They were simply offshoots, as you might remember, of the Puritan colony in Massachusetts. He granted them each a royal charter, giving them the liberty to govern themselves with *assemblies* chosen by *election* from among the free men of the colony. The Charter for Rhode Island also put into writing an important idea: all men should be free to follow whichever religion they choose or to practice their religion in the way that seems best to them. The charter says, "All . . . persons may, from time to time, and at all times hereafter, freely and fully have and enjoy . . . their own judgments and consciences, in matters of religious concernments." Thus it was that Rhode Island was the first colony to officially guarantee *freedom of religion*, which has been important in America since its earliest days.

As he neared the end of his life, Charles bestowed a royal charter upon another offshoot of Massachusetts, the colony of New Hampshire. Named for a lovely county in England, New Hampshire had been home to scattered fishermen and farmers for many years, its first settlers having put down roots in the 1620s. For most of those years, though, the colony had been governed by the colonial assembly in Massachusetts. It was a relationship that was often full of conflict, since the Puritans in Boston and the farmers in New Hampshire often had very different ideas about what was important or needful. Charles officially set New Hampshire apart in 1679 and gave it a governor of its own.

New Hampshire, Connecticut, Rhode Island: old colonies given new charters, and thus new, independent lives. Carolina, New York, New Jersey: freshly-established colonies, all of them gifts of the king. Although he sat on a faraway throne, a throne rocking unsteadily in the aftermath of a vicious Civil War, Charles II accomplished what he set out to do in North America: he made England's colonies stable and strong. But the king held one more debt in his hand, and we will see what became of that in the next chapter.

Chapter 13

Noble Experiments

Pennsylvania and Georgia

As King Charles II neared the end of his reign, he could look with satisfaction on the work he had done. The English colonies were prospering, and England with them. But, still, the king felt the burden of a debt unpaid. He wanted to do right by a certain Admiral of the Royal Navy, Sir William Penn, who had not only lent Charles a large sum of money but had also labored faithfully for many years, helping to secure the king's Restoration.

Admiral Penn had spent most of his life at sea. While he had served Oliver Cromwell and the Commonwealth, his sympathies remained with the exiled king, and his was the ship that brought Charles back to London to claim his restored throne. On that same voyage, Admiral Penn had commenced a friendship with James, the Duke of York, that would last for many years. Both the king and the duke were well-disposed toward the Admiral, and he, in turn, was depending on their good will. He needed help in the matter of his son, who was in considerable trouble.

This son was William Penn, named after his father. He had always been a serious, thoughtful boy. At the age of 15, he learned about the teachings of a man named George Fox, who said that all Christians should obey only the inner light of their own conscience, that warfare was evil, and that the church had no need for priests or bishops. He said that all men and women were equal, and that no man could hold himself above another man, not even the king. He bade all people to "tremble before the Word of the Lord." His teachings were hated by Puritans and *Anglicans* alike, who mockingly referred to Fox and his followers as "Quakers." To William Penn, though, the beliefs of the Quakers seemed reasonable and right, and, at the age of 22, he declared himself to be one of them.

This decision terrified his father. The Quakers were considered *heretics*: they were subject to scorn, imprisonment, public whippings, and even execution. Indeed, young William Penn was arrested several times, and, though on each occasion he was freed through the Admiral's wealth and public influence, his position became increasingly perilous. Admiral Penn was dying, and, with his father's death, William Penn would have no one to protect him. So, Admiral Penn wrote to the Duke of York, pleading for his help.

In response, both the duke and the king agreed to help young William Penn by shielding him from further prosecution. This promise secured, the old Admiral died in peace, and his son felt safe enough to marry the lady he had been courting and to continue to spread the Quaker message of simple worship and the equality of all men. But, as he settled into his marriage and mourned his father's loss, an idea was brewing in William Penn's head.

He wrote letters to the king and the duke, presenting his thoughts: since persecution of the Quakers is only increasing, causing sorrow and upheaval, why not allow the Quakers to go to the New World, where they can live in peace and cease to be a source of conflict in England?

To his surprise, the king responded with immense generosity: he signed a charter giving William Penn a truly enormous tract of land, west of New Jersey. This included a large chunk of New York, but the Duke was willing to part with it in return for Penn's promise that he would share any profits from the mining of silver or gold. With that, William Penn became the proprietor of the biggest colony in the New World. Joyously, he wrote, "It is a clear and just thing, and my God, that has given it to me through many difficulties, will, I believe, bless and make it the seed of a nation."

At first, he called his colony New Wales, and then Sylvania, from the Latin word for "forest." But the king insisted that the colony's name include a tribute to William's father, and be named Pennsylvania, for "Penn's Forest." Thus were the king's debts to the old Admiral finally satisfied.

William Penn set about advertising for settlers, promising generous grants of land and a government in which each man would be represented equally. Thousands responded, many of them Quakers, but others as well who sought a place where they could live in freedom. They traveled from Ireland, Wales, Holland, and Germany as well as from England; they came from the other colonies too, where Quakers had been treated with harshness and even cruelty.

William Penn made the voyage to the new colony in 1682. There, under a large oak tree, he met with the native people who inhabited that region, the Lenape. Even though he had a charter from the king, he wanted to be fair to the Natives and buy the land from them while still allowing them the right to travel freely and to hunt and fish as they had always done. Once he had settled this agreement with the Lenape, Penn laid out the boundaries of the colony's first city, which would be named Philadelphia, the "City of Brotherly Love." By 1700, just 20 years after its founding, Philadelphia was home to 10,000 people: many Quakers, to be sure, but also poor and downtrodden settlers attracted by Penn's promise that in Pennsylvania they could build a better life and farm their own land.

Penn himself wrote the colony's "Frame of Government," which guaranteed that all of Pennsylvania's leaders would come to power, and remain in power, only through the freely-given votes of the people. It included the Great Law: that no man or woman could be persecuted for his or her beliefs and that all religions were allowed. Penn also created a new idea: that this framework of government could be *amended*, or changed, if the people voted to do so. The colony was meant to be a "holy experiment" where people could live together in friendship and peace.

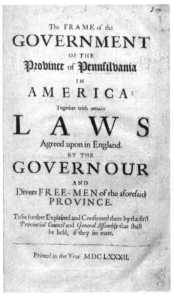

William Penn's "Frame of Government"

Some 50 years later, another experimental colony would come into being, England's last. In 1732, the land between the Savannah and Altamaha Rivers, south and west of Charles Town in Carolina, was given to 21 worthy men. They were *philanthropists*, which means that they sought to use their money and time for the good of others. They dreamed of building a refuge for people in England who had been sent to debtor's prison, which means they had been thrust into jail because they could not pay back money they owed to merchants or moneylenders. The leader of these philanthropists was an Army General, James Oglethorpe. He had persuaded the king to grant them land in North America by presenting it as a two-fold blessing: England would be gaining another southern colony to stand fast against Spanish Florida, and England's worthy poor would be given a chance to rebuild their lives, which had been ruined by debt and imprisonment.

In 1733 General Oglethorpe and 114 colonists arrived in their new home, which they had named Georgia after the king who had given them their charter, George II. The General set to work at once, putting into action the plans that he and his fellow philanthropists had carefully crafted. They wanted to encourage small farms and tightly knit villages, rather like what the Puritans were doing in New England, and to accomplish this they limited each colonist to 50 acres of farmland where they were encouraged to plant vineyards and mulberry bushes for silkworms. Slavery was outlawed and rum was prohibited; General Oglethorpe and the other trustees envisioned a happy, peaceful colony of thrifty silk farmers and wine makers.

But, alas, this vision did not last. More and more people moved into Georgia, and they wanted to grow tobacco, rice, and cotton, crops that must be harvested and tended by many hands. By 1750, the ban on slavery was lifted, and the unhappy trade in their fellow humans quickly became commonplace among Georgians. In the end, only one of General Oglethorpe's purposes for the colony was fulfilled: it was indeed a firm guard against any northward expansion by the Spaniards in Florida. But as an experiment in generosity, it ultimately failed. By 1754, the philanthropists' charter had expired, and the land became the king's once again. No more freed prisoners working their small vineyards: Georgia became a center of colonial trade, with huge *plantations*—large farms focused on growing one or two profitable crops—harvesting enormous quantities of rice, cotton, indigo, and timber.

With the addition of Georgia and Pennsylvania, England had secured for herself a strong foothold in the New World, far outpacing the colonial efforts of either France or Spain. Thirteen colonies now linked arms together along the eastern coast of the continent, providing a home to many kinds of people. Some had come for religious freedom, some to gain what wealth they could. Some had arrived in chains as the scourge of slavery spread its evil stain. Some had given up everything to make the journey, their faces turned with hope toward a new world where a poor man could own his small parcel of land and make his own way in the world, beholden to no one but himself and God. Some came to build a haven for others, and those others arrived in wave after grateful wave.

They still thought of themselves as Englishmen and claimed loyalty to the English king, but, already, they were becoming something else. Far from their home country, their minds and hearts were turned toward the unique adventure of settling a new land. Together, as they lived and worked, they were becoming Americans.

Chapter 14

The Charter Oak

The Seeds of Independence in the Colonies

If you were to go for a mountain hike in the late spring when the snow has finally surrendered its grip, you might come across a meadow set apart from the trees and glowing in the sun. It would be filled with wildflowers blossoming in drifts among the grass. The flowers are many different kinds—sage, violets, lilies, bluebells—and their colors blend together into an exquisite garden, but it is a garden that no human plotted and no hands planned. It grew up haphazardly, each flower independent of the rest. It is only when they've bloomed and matured that the scene comes together as one glorious display.

In much the same way, England's American colonies, which would one day make a united whole, began as separate, haphazard parts. Some had been founded by trading companies; some were owned directly by the king; some had proprietors who were friends of the king. Some, like the Puritan colony of Massachusetts, established one official church; some, like Pennsylvania, allowed churches of any kind. The colonies of northern New England engaged mostly in shipbuilding and fishing; others immersed themselves in trading, with ships sailing out from Philadelphia and New York City laden with wheat and corn, furs and indigo. In the southernmost colonies, large plantations grew tobacco and cotton.

The Virginia House of Burgesses in Williamsburg, Virginia

Despite their differences, each colony's government was similar, based upon the rules set up in the charters granted by the king. A governor represented the colony's owner, whether that was the king, a proprietor, or a trading company. A council of colonist landowners was appointed by the governor to give him advice. Finally, an assembly, elected by the local people, was charged with making the colony's laws. The governor was meant to be the strongest power in this arrangement, since he had to enforce in the colonies all of the decrees of the king and Parliament back in England. The governor could, with one stroke of his pen, *annul*—or cancel—any law that the colonial assembly created. But as the years went by and the colonies prospered, most of the power in North America was actually wielded by the assemblies. They were the ones who collected taxes from the people and, thus, controlled the money in the colony, including the money used to pay the governor's wages. And they were fully in charge of making colonial laws; the governor could not force them to enact any law that they opposed. These laws, and the assemblies who made them, meant that the colonies ruled themselves, despite the governor's authority, and so the colonies grew very accustomed to the liberty of self-government.

However, back during the years of Charles II, as he was strengthening and establishing colonies in the New World, he also sought more control over them. The king's main concern was trade; he wanted the colonies to continue to produce all of their valuable trade goods, and he also wanted the colonies to buy cloth and tools and paint, all manufactured in England. To tighten its grip on colonial trade, England's Parliament had passed several laws in the middle of the seventeenth century called the Navigation Acts. These laws declared that the colonies could sell their tobacco and sugar only to England, that only English ships could bring foreign goods to America, and that ships which traded with the New World must have mostly English crews. These rules meant that the colonies did very little trade with any country but England, and, as you can imagine, it infuriated the colonial farmers and merchants. They wanted to sell their sugar and tobacco all over the world.

And then, in 1685, Charles II died. His brother, the Duke of York, became King James II. Determined to embrace the colonies even more closely, James decreed that six of them— New York, New Jersey, Massachusetts, Rhode Island, New Hampshire, and Connecticut—would all be joined together into one great colony called the Dominion of New England. All of the colonies' charters were revoked, which means that those six colonies could no longer govern themselves. Instead, they would all be under the authority of one royal governor appointed by the king, who would rule without any council or colonial assembly.

The appointed royal governor, Sir Edmund Andros, arrived in Boston in 1686. The power he'd been given was total and absolute, and he used it that way. He began to collect taxes, to enforce the hated Navigation Acts, to forbid town meetings, and to dispense with town and village governments. He declared that Boston's Puritans must allow worship services for the Church of England, which they were most unwilling to do, and even seized one of their churches for his own use. And, in the midst of all that, he insisted that the colonies surrender their charters to him, the governor of the Dominion of New England.

Some of the colonies, seeing no other choice, delivered up their charters at once. It seemed impossible to refuse, and yet one among them did: the little colony of Connecticut. As you might remember, Charles II had established the Connecticut Charter in 1662; it promised that the people of Connecticut had the right to govern themselves and to elect their own assemblies. The people of Connecticut could not accept the idea of losing that freedom; they refused to give up their charter. Finally, in October of 1687, Sir Edmund Andros rode to Hartford, Connecticut, bearing orders from the king himself: "Our Colony of Connecticut . . . shall be induced to make surrender of their Charter, our will and pleasure is, and we do hereby authorize and empower you, in our name, to receive such surrender, and to take our said Colony of Connecticut under your Government."

The colonists' elected governor, Robert Treat, met the governor at the edge of town and escorted him into the arranged meeting place, a tavern with a large central hall. There, a comfortable leather chair had been placed for Sir Edmund Andros, with all the colony's leaders seated before and around him. On a table before him lay the Charter, a roll of parchment pages tied with a leather string. Sir Edmund ordered the doors to be closed, and then, at his signal, his secretary stood and read out loud the king's orders: the charter must be surrendered, and the people of Connecticut must accept Sir Edmund as their ruler.

The legends about that day tell us what happened next. The leaders of the colony were determined to defend their charter, and, as the hours of the day passed, they pleaded and argued. We are loyal subjects of the king, they declared. What need is there to take our charter from us? There is every need, Sir Edmund replied, because the king has willed it so.

Dusk fell as they talked back and forth, and slowly the night deepened. Servants lit candles, and the light flickered on the weary faces of the colonists. They could see that their arguments were to no avail. Finally, Robert Treat stood. He picked up the charter, snipped the tie that held it closed, and unrolled it on the table. All the men in the room could see the image of Charles II inscribed there. Robert Treat pointed to it and said, "That Charter represents the accumulated efforts of the founders of this Colony and the toil and savings of their children. . . . Their blood was shed to save the homes guaranteed to them and their children by that Charter, and it is like giving up life itself to surrender it."

More voices were raised, the anger in the room blooming like a fiery rose. One of the men swept the candlesticks from the table in his passion. Instantly, the room was plunged into darkness. Shouts of alarm and confusion, thuds and bangs as men rushed here and there blindly, and over them all insistent cries for light! Someone finally produced a flint and steel, and someone else groped along the floor to find a fallen candle. When the flame lit, its small gleam kindled enough light for everyone to see that the table in front of Sir Edmund was bare. The charter had vanished!

What had happened, in fact, when the candles had gone out, was that one of the men nearest at hand had swept the charter up and, quickly, moving blindly in the dark, had passed it through a window to a bold young man named Joseph Wadsworth. He tucked it under his coat and ran to the edge of town, where, in a large field beside a fence, there grew a mighty oak tree, hollowed out by its immense age. Joseph Wadsworth thrust the rolled-up charter into the hollow trunk of the oak, certain that here was a place where Sir Edmund and his men would never think to search for it.

And so it was. Sir Edmund, no doubt red-faced with vexation, was forced to leave Hartford without Connecticut's charter. It would remain safe in the bosom of the oak tree.

Charter or no charter, Connecticut was made a part of the Dominion of New England, but it was a brief submission. Two years later, in 1689, James II was overthrown. In an event called the Glorious Revolution, he was replaced by his daughter, Queen Mary, and her Dutch husband, King William III. The powers of the king and queen were limited once again by Parliament.

This idea, that a king could be overthrown and replaced, was new and sometimes frightening. Also in 1689, in England, a philosopher named John Locke wrote a long book to defend the Glorious Revolution and explain why it had been necessary. He said that all people are given certain *natural rights*—that is, rights that are fixed and certain, rights that must be allowed to all—rights to life, liberty, and property. When a ruler tramples these rights and does not respect them, Locke said, his people have an additional right: the right to overthrow him and put another in his place.

The colonists agreed. When word of the overthrow of King James II reached the colonies, a mob of colonists cornered Sir Edmund Andros, and, declaring that they must and would have the government in their own hands, they arrested him and threw him into a jail in Boston. The colonial assemblies and local governments were re-established. The Connecticut charter emerged from its hiding place. It was used to govern Connecticut until the year 1818; and, even beyond, it has become an enduring symbol of free men's determination to remain free.

In Hartford, Connecticut, a sculpture adorns the north wall of the State Capitol building. It shows an oak tree, its sheltering limbs spread wide as Joseph Wadsworth slips the Connecticut Charter into its hollow trunk. The people of Connecticut still honor him for his courage and resourcefulness in defending the document that declared them to be free to govern themselves.

And the white oak is honored as Connecticut's state tree.

In Joseph Wadsworth and the colonists who faced Sir Edmund Andros, the seeds of self-government and freedom were in full bloom. In the rest of the colonies, those same seeds were taking root and growing fast.

Chapter 15

"Black Sam" Bellamy

Pirates and the Triangle Trade

On a fine morning early in the year 1717, the ship *Whydah* gracefully pierced the waves as she sailed the Caribbean Sea between the islands of Hispaniola and Cuba. But her captain, Lawrence Prince, took no pleasure in her swift passage, nor in the sparkling sunlight of the lovely day. His gaze was fixed anxiously to the rear where, on the horizon, another ship could be seen, the same ship that had been relentlessly pursuing the *Whydah* for three days and nights. By the time the sun rested overhead at noon, Captain Prince would be able to see her clearly: a stout galley bearing the name *Sultana* and flying a flag that chilled the blood, a black flag with a set of crossed bones and a cheerfully-grinning skull, a flag flown only by pirates.

As the *Sultana* hove nearer, the stark black mouths of its cannons leered threateningly, and, soon, one of those mouths coughed out a smoking cannonball: a warning shot. His crew was unwilling to risk their lives in a cutthroat battle with pirates, so Captain Prince ordered a flag of his own run up the mast: the white flag of surrender. The *Sultana* snugged itself up close to its prey, and the pirate captain stepped aboard, a fabulous figure dressed in a velvet coat and silver-buckled shoes with four ornate pistols tucked into the sash at his waist. He was "Black

Sam" Bellamy, so called because, unlike other men of the day, he refused to wear a powdered white wig; his own black locks were tied back with a black ribbon. He bowed to Captain Prince and accepted the *Whydah*'s surrender with exquisite courtesy while the captured crew murmured and craned their necks to get a better look at him.

Samuel Bellamy had been born in England and was left motherless at a young age. Like many young men in such situations, he'd chosen to try his luck at sea and eventually had found his way to New England in the year 1715. There, on the shores of Cape Cod, he had met a pretty lady named Maria Hallett and sought to woo her. But her family saw no future for her with a poor young sailor, and so he'd left again, this time to make his fortune in the Caribbean Sea by salvaging shipwrecks full of Spanish treasure. The Spaniards had wrenched thousands of pounds of gold and silver from their conquests of the Inca and the Aztec empires, and the ships bearing this glittering wealth sometimes came to grief in the wild waves of Caribbean storms. If a man could find the grave of such a ship and risk the dangerous dive down to sift through its wreckage, he might be able to amass a tidy fortune.

But such was not the fate of Sam Bellamy. His grand plan came to nothing, for he could not find a wreck to plunder, and, at last, desperate and determined, he took to piracy.

A pirate, of course, is an ocean-going thief, one who chases down and robs ships. Starting very shortly after the year of Columbus's voyage, scores of pirates roamed the waters of the New World—the Caribbean Sea, the Gulf of Mexico, the Atlantic Ocean—preying upon the merchant ships and treasure *galleons*. Some of them were *privateers*, pirates who had been given permission from their king to attack the ships of other nations, but most were willing to fall upon any ship who crossed their paths. Pirate ships carried large crews, sufficient numbers to overwhelm their victims, but they were interested mainly in plunder and thievery rather than pitched battle. Sailing close, they would fire one warning shot, hoping for a quick surrender. If their victims decided to resist, the boldest and fiercest of the pirate crew would leap aboard, swinging their curved cutlasses and lobbing smoke grenades. When the ship had been subdued, the pirates would load all of its cargo into their own vessel, or, if the captured ship were swifter or larger, they would take it for themselves and likely offer the captured crew the option of joining them.

And such was the case with the *Whydah*. She was a sleek, beautiful ship armed with 18 cannon. Sam Bellamy was eager to claim her as his own, but first he must remove the extra weight that was loading her down. Her hull was filled with boxy hold-rooms and bare plank beds, for the *Whydah* was a merchant ship built for an ugly purpose: to carry slaves.

A slave is someone held captive and forced to labor without pay or liberty, a practice that has existed in many cultures around the world since nearly the beginning of time as evidence of the cruelty that humans can sometimes practice upon one another. In the New World, slaves worked the fields of large plantations, harvesting the sugar or the cotton, brewing up the rum or the molasses. Many of them were Natives, forced to labor for their conquerors, and many more of them came from far afield: Africa.

The *Whydah* had left England in the winter of 1716 and made her way south to Africa, to the port of Ouidah in the modern-day nation of Benin, from which she took her name. Her purpose there was to pick up captive Africans. Most of these were prisoners of war, the losers in local conflicts between tribal chieftains. Every year, thousands of Africans were loaded onto ships in Ouidah. When the *Whydah* left the port, she carried more than 300 captives, and she delivered them across the Atlantic to a life of labor and servitude in the Americas.

This journey, which took eight weeks or so, was called the Middle Passage, because it was the second leg of a circular route, the Triangle Trade, with the Caribbean at its heart: from Europe to Africa to America and then back to Europe again. Europe sent cloth and tools to Africa; which in turn exported ivory, salt, and gold back to Europe and sent captive slaves west, to the New World. The Caribbean islands and the lands of Central America shipped sugar and coffee to Europe along with gold and silver, while the North American colonies sent their cotton and tobacco eastward as well. In this constantly swirling whirlpool of ships and wealth, the pirates circled as well, like vultures.

The *Whydah* had offloaded her cargo of captives in Jamaica, and her hold was packed now with the goods of the New World: gold, silver, sugar, and spices. After removing the slave holds, Sam Bellamy and his crew stuffed her further still, packing her stores with all of their accumulated loot from the *Sultana* and adding 10 more cannon to her decks. Then, assuming command of the *Whydah,* Bellamy offered the captured men a choice: go now with your captain aboard the *Sultana,* or stay here with us and choose the pirate's life. Twelve or so of the men agreed to join the *Whydah's* crew.

This may seem doubly surprising to you. A pirate captain allowing his prisoners to sail away freely? Some of those same prisoners willingly choosing to become outlaw pirates? It was a risky life, for a pirate captured by the land-going authorities would surely be put on trial and hanged. But it was a life of freedom on the open sea with promise of great, if ill-gotten, reward. From their raucous Caribbean ports in places like Port Royal in Jamaica or Tortuga in Haiti, pirates rampaged far up the North American coast and east across the Atlantic, attacking the ships of Europe as they engaged in the Triangle Trade.

Those dozen men who chose to join Bellamy's pirate crew found themselves part of a varied lot. There were sailors from all over Europe and every one of the colonies; there were freed slaves and African tribesmen; the ship's navigator was a 16-year-old Native from Central America named John Julian. There was young John King, just 11 years old, who had insisted upon joining Bellamy's crew when the pirates had attacked the ship on which he was a passenger. As members of the crew, each of them had an equal share of the shipboard work as well as the loot they stole. Together, they called themselves "Robin Hood's Men," for they saw Sam Bellamy as a heroic figure, stealing from wealthy merchants and kings. Bellamy himself viewed the merchant companies with scorn. "They vilify us, the scoundrels do," he once declared, "when there is only this difference: they rob the poor under the cover of law, forsooth, and we plunder the rich under the protection of our own courage."

Turning his new flagship northward toward Carolina and then New England, Sam Bellamy became a fearsome force to be reckoned with. Over the course of the next few months, he attacked 53 ships, taking loot and plunder that would be worth more than 100 million of today's dollars. He was the terror of the colonial seas and the richest pirate the world had ever seen.

But his end came soon and with a vengeance. Turning at last toward Cape Cod and a reunion with Maria Hallett, Bellamy and the *Whydah* were caught in a ferocious storm on the evening of April 26, 1717. It was a *nor'easter*—a cyclone over the North Atlantic whose winds howl from the northeast—and this one is still considered one of the worst storms to ever strike Cape Cod. Strong and fleet the *Whydah* was, but she was no match for the brute force of the storm. She was hurled against a sandbar; her heavy cannons broke loose, her mast snapped in two, and her cargo—all those thousands of pounds of gold and silver and ivory and indigo—smashed through her hull. She sank in minutes into the frigid waves, and, though the beaches of Cape Cod were only 500 feet away, she took her crew down with her. Out of the 142 men aboard, only two escaped—a carpenter and the navigator, John Julian.

For another 70 years or so after the *Whydah's* sinking, pirates continued to hound the Triangle Trade until the nations of the

New World grew serious and stern about hunting the pirates down and ending them. But for 200 years, pirates haunted the oceans under the black flag, and "Black Sam" Bellamy was the richest of them all.

He never returned to Maria Hallett; he was lost forever and his tons of stolen treasure with him. The *Whydah* remained buried in her sandy grave for many years until she was finally rediscovered in 1984. Slowly her treasures are being recovered, still to this day; you can see many of them for yourself should you ever visit Provincetown, Massachusetts. But you cannot see the bones of Black Sam Bellamy; they were buried by the storm.

Chapter 16

"We Shall Know Better"

The French and Indian War

If you were to travel west from New York City, into the Appalachian Mountains and the green, hilly lands beyond, you would find yourself in what is today the state of Pennsylvania. There, the city of Pittsburgh lies cradled between the arms of two rivers, which join there to form the Ohio River, one of America's great waterways. The Ohio River flows for a thousand miles westward through a wide, rich valley, eventually to empty itself into the mighty, rolling waters of the Mississippi. One of America's first presidents, Thomas Jefferson, wrote that the Ohio is "the most beautiful river on earth. Its current gentle, waters clear, and bosom smooth and unbroken."

The Native Americans who lived along its lovely waters agreed, calling it *O-hee-yo*, "the good river." To the French, who traveled its length in their ever-broadening search for beaver pelts, it was the beautiful river, *la Belle Rivierè*. Indeed, the river and the lands it watered were admired and coveted by all who saw them.

The French claimed the Ohio River Valley, but nevertheless in 1749, King George II of England granted a huge portion of that region to a new trading company. Formed in Virginia, the Ohio Company planned to bring settlers into the valley to farm and trade with the native people there. A wave of enterprising Virginians flowed up and over the mountains, eager to make new homes in the Ohio River's gentle valley.

But the French viewed their arrival as nothing more than a greedy land grab by the English. The French had been traveling through the Ohio Valley for many years, though they had built no settlements there. As was the case for most of New France, the Frenchmen viewed the valley as a source of trading goods, and so they had pushed ever southward, concerned only with trapping beavers and buying and selling with the Natives. They had no desire to build homes there, but they also had no intention of sharing this rich country. Angrily, they responded to the Virginians' arrival by slapping together a string of new forts along the river.

This rivalry between England and France was nothing new. Since 1689, the two nations had been fighting for dominion on land and supremacy on the ocean. Though at first these wars had been confined to Europe, they began to break out in the New World as well. In their struggles to overcome one another, both nations sometimes called upon colonial soldiers and *militia*— citizen soldiers—to join their battles, and both nations formed alliances with the Native Americans—the French making partnerships with the Huron and the Algonquin peoples, and the English allying themselves with the Iroquois.

The angry fort-building by the French, in turn, provoked the governor of Virginia, Robert Dinwiddie. He sent a small party of Virginia militiamen to build a fort of their own at the strategic fork where the Allegheny and Monongahela Rivers joined to form the Ohio River. Then, to drive his point home, he dispatched another small force, eight soldiers strong, led by a young, 21-year-old major named George Washington. His mission was to warn the French that the Virginians had every right, with a land grant from the English king, to settle in the Ohio Valley. The French must leave, and that was that.

You can probably guess the French response. When Major Washington reported to Governor Dinwiddie that the French refused to go, the governor sent him right back again, this time with a larger force of armed Virginians, a group of Iroqouis warriors, and a new mission: protect the militiamen as they constructed their fort.

Unfortunately, as they drew near, they found to their dismay that the Virginian builders had been driven away by a large party of French soldiers. The Frenchmen had torn down the foundations of the Virginians' fort and erected a stronghold of their own that they had named Fort Duquesne (doo KAYN), after the French governor of Canada. Stymied but undeterred, Washington retreated to await reinforcements.

The very next day, he and his men learned that a party of French soldiers was approaching on a foray into the forest. Washington moved quickly to confront them and learn their intentions, but before he could do so, a shot was fired, a short battle ensued, and most of the Frenchmen were killed or captured. Fearing a return attack, Washington hastily built a shelter, Fort Necessity. And, just as he had foreseen, the French and their Huron allies attacked the fort about a month later, on July 3, 1754. The Virginians and their young leader were quickly overwhelmed. With more than a third of his men killed, Washington surrendered the fort and faced the long, sad walk back to Virginia, the loser in the first battle of what would come to be known in the New World as the French and Indian War.

Determined to prevail against the stubborn French, England sent one of her best officers to the colonies: Major General Edward Braddock, who landed in Virginia in 1755 with two large regiments of English soldiers. As Commander in Chief, Braddock was given the task of pushing the French out of the Ohio River Valley, and, in pursuit of that goal, he aimed his troops toward Fort Duquesne. What a glorious sight they were, the valiant English, as they journeyed into the American wilderness, marching four abreast in their brilliant red coats, flags snapping in the wind, drums beating in time with their footsteps! Young George Washington, who had been sent to accompany Braddock with a regiment of Virginia militiamen, was struck by the martial beauty of the scene.

But Washington also realized that those bright coats and loud drums made the English soldiers vulnerable. He had faced Native warriors; he knew what might be awaiting them there in the forest. General Braddock did not. He was accustomed to the broad, open battlefields of Europe, where the soldiers advanced upon one another in orderly, straight lines. But here, when the attack came, it came in a narrow valley, with the French and their Native allies firing from behind trees and from the shadows, the Natives' terrifying war cries erupting from every side. The English soldiers panicked, uncertain what to do or where to fire; Washington would later say that they "broke and ran as sheep pursued by dogs." When Washington and his Virginians melted into the trees to take cover, the English began firing at them by mistake, thinking them to be Frenchmen. In the chaos and confusion, General Braddock was felled by a gunshot. One legend claims that he was killed by a Virginia soldier who was hoping to stop the wild and reckless shooting.

As he lay dying, Braddock called for Washington and gave him the silken sash that he had worn during the battle. "Who would have thought it?" he said. "We shall better know how to deal with them another time." And, perhaps in recognition of this painful lesson, George Washington kept the sash with him for the rest of his life. You can still see it today, should you ever visit Washington's home at Mount Vernon in Virginia.

But did they know better? At first, the tide of the war seemed to be flowing against the English. Braddock had been easily defeated, and the French were launching ships to bring soldiers and supplies into Canada. France's Native American allies were ravaging through the colonial settlements, burning and killing.

But then a new leader came to power in England. His name was William Pitt; he became *prime minister* of the English Parliament in 1756, which means that he was the head of the government, responsible for running the country in the king's name. After considering the course of England's history of wars with France, which encompassed nearly the entire globe by this point, he knew what needed to be done. "I can save this country," he declared, "and nobody else can." He had deduced that the key to English victory was to concentrate on the war in the New World. To that end, he ordered the British Navy to cut off all French access to North America to barricade its ports in Canada and prevent the landing of new troops and supplies. And he sent many, many more soldiers of his own, the best that England had, and her best commanders: Generals Jeffrey Amherst and James Wolfe.

By 1758 the tide began to turn. In Canada, English troops captured Montreal and Louisbourg, two important fortresses. They marched to Fort Duquesne with such a large force that the outnumbered French fled at once, leaving the fort in flames behind them. The English rebuilt it and renamed it Fort Pitt after the English prime minister. Today, it has grown into the city of Pittsburgh in Pennsylvania.

Finally, in 1759, the English were ready to strike the killing blow. Under the command of James Wolfe, the English troops marched up into Canada along the St. Lawrence River and surrounded the fortress of Quebec, which was the capital and chief city of New France, founded by Samuel de Champlain all those years ago. Perched atop steep cliffs and surrounded by thick walls, Quebec seemed unconquerable. But, after two months of trying, General Wolfe and his men found a way to climb up the cliffs behind the city. During the night of September 12, they silently ascended. When dawn lifted night's curtain the next morning, the French were startled to find the English army arrayed for battle just outside Quebec's walls. When the French soldiers emerged to defend their city, the English overcame them in less than an hour. The French were forced to leave Quebec and, thus, all of Canada, in the hands of the English.

The war limped on for three more years, but with the victory at Quebec, England had prevailed. In 1761, a new king ascended the throne, George III. He was interested above all in peace and removed Pitt as prime minister despite his great success in the war. By 1763 England was ready to accept the surrender offered by France. France's chief ally, Spain, too, was weary of conflict after being soundly defeated by the English in Cuba and the Philippines. Representatives of the three nations gathered in Paris and there signed the Treaty of Paris of 1763, which ended the French and Indian War.

England gained the most. The Treaty gave to England all of France's possessions in the New World: Canada, of course, but also all of the lands France had claimed between the Appalachian Mountains and the east bank of the Mississippi River, from the Ohio River Valley south to the Gulf of Mexico. For her part in the war, Spain was required to give up Florida.

Truly, at this moment in history, England reigned supreme. She had defeated her enemies and won for herself a global empire, with colonies in Asia, in Africa, in the Caribbean Sea, and, especially, in North America. Surely the years to come would only bring more triumphs. Surely England would continue to rule North America, and her colonies there would bring her ever more wealth and power.

Surely, for England, nothing could possibly go wrong.

But England's actions during the French and Indian War would result not in a grand empire in America but rather in the loss of everything that she held there. In the hearts of her American colonists, England was sowing the seeds of revolution, and those seeds would soon take root and begin to grow.

Chapter 17

Farewell, Acadia

Exiles in Louisiana and a Meeting in Albany

L et us step away, for just a moment, from the wide shores of North America and whisk ourselves across the Atlantic Ocean. Let's find the land of Greece where it lies many miles to the south and east of England and France. Greece is almost split in two by the waters of the Mediterranean Sea: its northern half is a broad stretch of land reaching downward and, below that, a peninsula shaped almost like a hand. This is the Peloponnese, and at its very center you can find a softly beautiful region called Arcadia.

In the ancient myths of Greece, Arcadia was the realm of the god Pan, who loved the wild forest groves and green meadows. Surrounded by mountains and filled with wooded glens and hilly pastures, Arcadia was a refuge, a place of unspoiled beauty and nature's peace, a home to shepherds and gardeners.

And so, when Giovanni Verrazzano, whom you might remember from Chapter 7, created a map of his wanderings along America's uppermost coast, he designated the whole region north of Virginia as "Arcadia" as a tribute to its wild, peaceful beauty. When New France came into being, and its various regions took their names, Samuel de Champlain and his mapmakers followed Verrazzano's lead and bestowed the name, minus its "r," onto the parts of New France furthest to the east, where the Atlantic Ocean laps the shores—the same lands that the Vikings, centuries before, had christened Vinland. Today, this region is divided up: part of it is in the state of Maine, and the rest is Canada's Maritime provinces: New Brunswick, Nova Scotia, and Prince Edward Island. But back then, in the earliest years of New France, it was all the land of Acadia.

The French had made a settlement there in 1605, even before the English had founded Jamestown, and the settlers had made Acadia a lovely place with farms and fishing villages and gardens. But over the many long years of wars between England and France, Acadia had become a much fought-over prize, and, by 1710, she had been conquered and made into an English territory.

However, her people still spoke the French language and thought fondly of France as their mother country. They had no loyalty to England; indeed, when the English asked them to swear an oath of allegiance to England's king, the Acadians refused. And so, when the French and Indian War began in 1754, the English looked upon the Acadians with deep suspicion. The French needed to bring soldiers and supplies into Canada, after all, and what better place to do so than the beaches and ports of Acadia? The English wanted to secure their hold on that land and prevent the French from using it, and they decided to achieve that goal in a way both simple and very cruel: they emptied Acadia of all its people.

Some 14,000 men, women, and children lived in Acadia; and over the course of 10 years, from 1755 to 1765, all of them were forced to leave. The English soldiers raided their farms and houses, herding the people onto ships waiting in the harbor. At first, the Acadians were sent south to the American colonies; they gathered there in the port cities, lived in poverty in ragged houses, and still spoke French, longing for home. When it became clear to the English that the exiled Acadians were merely biding their time and making plans to return to Canada, they began to send them yet farther away, to France itself.

Sorrow accompanied them wherever they went; farms and livelihoods were lost forever, families were separated, ships sank with hundreds of Acadians lost into the sea.

Finally, a gleam of hope appeared after the French and Indian War ended. The Acadians still left in America turned their eyes toward Louisiana, the enormous territory still held by France along the western shore of the Mississippi River. Slowly, the sad exiles made their way there, traveling west to the Mississippi and south along its broad banks until they reached its wide mouth and the delta there. They became the largest group in that region, and over the years their name, Acadian, changed and evolved into a new name: Cajun. You can find their descendants living there today in the state of Louisiana.

Acadia had been a haven, a place of beauty and peace, but that peace was ripped asunder by the English in their insistence on winning the French and Indian War. And it was not the Acadian people alone who lost their peaceful refuge; others met that same fate. When news of the Treaty of Paris of 1763 was brought to them—the news that England had been given all of the land west of the Appalachians—the Native tribes in those lands were frightened and appalled. One of their chiefs, a man named Pontiac, said in protest, "The French never conquered us, neither did they purchase a foot of our Country, nor have they a right to give it to you." But the English thought otherwise; English soldiers occupied all of the forts that the French had built in the Ohio Valley, and more and more English settlers traveled over the mountains to build homes and farms. Some of the Natives rose up in desperate rebellion, attacking the forts in the Ohio Valley and raiding colonial settlements, destroying homes and killing several thousand colonists. In an effort to stop this violence, England's King George III gave out a decree called the Proclamation of 1763. It called for 10,000 English soldiers to stay permanently in the colonies as an army of protection, and it also reserved the land west of the Appalachian Mountains for the Native people, forbidding any more settlement there by colonists.

This was meant to restore peace by calming the Natives' fears, but, of course, it made the settlers furious. The French and Indian War had been dreadful for England's colonists. Though it was a war between two great European nations, it was the Americans who had suffered the most. It was the farmers and traders and settlers throughout the colonies who were mercilessly attacked, their homes burned, and their families murdered. The war had cost many colonists their lives, their homes, and their fortunes; and now the king, far away in England, was telling them that they could not make new homes and new lives in the lands to the west. The colonists simply refused to accept this, and many of them moved over the mountains anyway.

And so the Natives of the Ohio Valley, like the Acadians, would become exiles and wanderers.

Refuge and peace are easily lost and must be defended. The people of the 13 colonies, too, had been refugees: from religious persecution, from poverty, from imprisonment. The colonists recognized that they could not simply stand back and rely on England to defend them, but for most of the years since their founding, each colony had thought of itself as a separate, individual place, responsible only for itself. The danger and threat of the French and Indian War inspired the colonies, for the first time, to attempt to work together as one. In June of 1754, during the first year of the war, representatives from seven of the colonies met in Albany, New York. They invited 150 Iroquois chieftains to join them. At first, this meeting was meant to be a simple discussion about how they might work together to defend themselves from the threat of France and her Native American allies and how they might best make alliances with the Natives themselves. But the meeting in Albany quickly grew into something else entirely, and that was because of the ideas burning in the brain of a representative from Pennsylvania, a man named Benjamin Franklin.

Benjamin Franklin was a printer by profession, but, by habit and personality, he was a thinker and an observer. He had spent a great deal of time among the Iroquois tribes, and he had observed how they had organized themselves into a *confederation*—a collection of independent groups joined under one government. At the Albany meeting, Franklin proposed that the colonies do the same: they should form a single government for all of England's North American colonies, with a president appointed by the king who would preside over a council of elected *representatives*. This council—a *congress*, Franklin called it—could meet once a year to devise laws concerning colonial matters.

Franklin had been thinking about this idea for some time. He had devised and printed a cartoon to illustrate it: it showed a serpent on a white background, its body cut into pieces, and each piece labeled as one of the colonies. "Join, or Die," it said, in stark, black letters.

Benjamin Franklin's "Join, or Die" cartoon

Franklin knew that the colonies were an Arcadia that could be easily lost. *Join or die,* he pleaded with the Albany *delegates. We must stand together.*

But the time for this idea was not yet ripe. The individual colonies rejected Franklin's confederation, unwilling to give up their self-rule for one united government. And back in England, King George utterly refused to consider such a plan.

But the idea did not die. The picture of the divided serpent did not fade away, because, when the French and Indian War ended, the threats to colonial peace did not. The colonists' refuge was still in danger, not now from France or Spain but from its own mother country. England herself would become the enemy, and, to face her, the colonists would indeed have to join together or lose their own Arcadia forever.

Chapter 18

Poor Richard

The Brilliant Life of Benjamin Franklin

From the day of his birth, Benjamin Franklin's life was lit by fire and by freedom.

His father, Josiah Franklin, was a candlemaker in the city of Boston, spending his days shaping tallow and wick to create light for his neighbors' homes. Josiah's wife was Abiah Folger, a descendant of the Puritans who had fled from England, following the light of freedom to America. Together, Josiah and Abiah had many children; young Benjamin was their fifteenth, born on January 17 of the year 1706.

With such a large family, Josiah and Abiah sometimes found money scarce. Though their dearest wish for Benjamin was that he would become a clergyman, such a profession required years of schooling, and the Franklin family could not afford the cost. Benjamin attended school for only two years, where he learned to read and write; by the age of 10, he had left the schoolroom behind and was working in his father's candle shop. It seemed, perhaps, that he would follow in his father's footsteps, quietly dipping candles and selling them to the citizens of Boston.

But learning to read had set off sparks in young Benjamin Franklin's heart and mind. He read whenever he could: stories of adventure, scientific theories, atlases of geography, the plays of Shakespeare, the musings of Greek philosophers, the solemn truths of the Bible. The love of learning burned hot within him, and he thirsted for a larger life outside the walls of the candle shop. He began to talk of going to sea and sailing the world's oceans.

But his parents did not wish such a future for him, and so, at age 12, Benjamin was sent to live with his elder brother James who was a printer. With a large press that he had brought all the way from Germany, James printed advertisements and announcements for his customers, and, most importantly of all, he printed a weekly newsletter for the city of Boston: *The New-England Courant,* one of the very first American newspapers.

Though he was working hard in his brother's printshop, learning the fascinating ways of the huge mechanical press, Benjamin Franklin's mind was still afire with ideas. He continued to read incessantly, but now he began to write as well, papers overflowing with the thoughts that filled his head. His brother, who was often very stern, refused to even consider printing these writings. So Benjamin resorted to disguising his handwriting and writing his ideas in the form of letters from an imaginary middle-aged widow named Silence Dogood. He slipped the letters under the printshop's door, as if the mysterious Mrs. Dogood had walked by and delivered them. Then he waited with bated breath while James read them, a thoughtful frown on his stern face. When James declared them good enough to publish in the newspaper, Benjamin could barely repress a shout of triumph. "Silence Dogood" quickly became a favorite with the newspaper's readers; no one suspected for a single moment that the writer was actually James Franklin's young apprentice. When James was thrown in jail for a month in 1722 for publishing an essay unflattering to Massachusetts's royal governor, Benjamin wrote in the voice of Mrs. Dogood quoting the *London Journal:* "Without freedom of thought, there can be no such thing as wisdom; and no such thing as public liberty, without freedom of speech."

But despite these successes, Benjamin chafed under his brother's heavy hand. One day, after he and James had quarreled, Benjamin ran away from the printshop and boarded a ship bound down the coast to Philadelphia, in the colony of Pennsylvania.

You will remember Philadelphia, the City of Brotherly Love, founded by William Penn 50 years before. It was a bustling place with abundant opportunities for a young man to make something of himself. Benjamin Franklin arrived on Philadelphia's docks with only one dollar in his pocket, but he soon found work in a printshop doing the tasks he already knew so well. He found lodging in the home of a gentleman named John Read whose pretty daughter Deborah had already caught Ben's eye. Even though he was only 17, and she but 15, he asked her to be his wife; her parents, though, would not consent.

Though he failed to win the hand of Deborah Read, his fine work and nimble mind brought him to the attention of Pennsylvania's governor, Sir William Keith. The governor declared that Philadelphia needed a newspaper, and he proposed to send Benjamin to London to buy a printing press. Alas, though, he neglected to supply any money, and Benjamin was forced to stay in London for four years, working and saving every coin he could. To his dismay, while he was gone, Deborah Read was persuaded by her mother to marry someone else.

This was a hard loss, but, as always, Benjamin found comfort in books. His time in London only increased his love for words and ideas. When he returned to Philadelphia in 1726, he formed an organization called the *Junto*; it was a group of businessmen and craftsmen who met together to read and discuss and argue their thoughts. Because books were expensive and hard to acquire, Benjamin proposed an excellent idea: a collection of books available to them all, bought and cared for with a yearly membership fee. Thus it was that Benjamin Franklin started the first subscription library in Philadelphia and hired a man named Louis Timothee to become America's first professional librarian.

But it was not enough for Benjamin Franklin to discuss his ideas with a single group of men. He wanted to reach further. In 1728 he started his own newspaper, the *Pennsylvania Gazette*. He viewed his work as a printer to be a duty and a service, not only to his fellow men but also to God, because he felt strongly that a person possesses good virtues only if he acts upon them, and by printing his newspaper full of worthy advice and stories of righteous deeds, he was putting his own virtues—his love for learning, his desire to help others—into action. For that same reason, in 1733, Benjamin's printing press began producing an *almanac*, which is a kind of magazine published yearly and filled with useful information. If you'd like to know when the moon will be full six months from now or when is the best time to plant pumpkins for an October harvest, you could consult an almanac.

Benjamin's almanac was special, though. In addition to all the useful facts, it also contained advice for living virtuously, often written as short, catchy sayings that were easy to remember: "No gains without pains"; "Diligence is the Mother of Good-Luck"; "One *Today* is worth two *Tomorrows*"; "The Proud hate Pride—in others." And, perhaps remembering his success with Silence Dogood, Benjamin published this work under the name of Richard Saunders and called it *Poor Richard's Almanack*. The Almanac was an enormous success, selling many copies across the length and breadth of the colonies, and more and more people came to know this wise Poor Richard and his creator, Benjamin Franklin.

Benjamin had prospered in his family life as well. He discovered that Deborah Read, whom he had loved since he was a lad of 17, had been abandoned by her husband, a scapegrace rascal who had run away to the West Indies and died there. In 1730, eight years after they met, Deborah and Benjamin were finally married. They would go on to raise three children together.

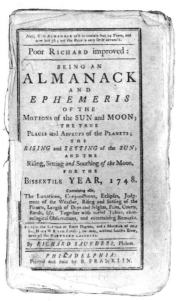

Poor Richard's Almanack

With his wife and home secure, Benjamin felt that the time had come to involve himself more directly in the public life of his city. In 1736 he started Philadelphia's first volunteer firefighting company; the year after that he was made the city's postmaster, in charge of mail delivery. Within the next few years, he helped to found the city's first hospital and the academy that would eventually become the University of Pennsylvania. By 1749 he had been appointed Pennsylvania's Justice of the Peace; two years later he was elected to the colony's governing assembly. As the French and Indian War loomed, he organized a militia to help protect Pennsylvania from attacks by Native Americans allied to the French. By 1753 he had become so well-known and well-respected that he was asked by England's Parliament to take charge of the postal system for all 13 colonies and became postmaster not just for Philadelphia, but for everyone. In 1757 he was sent to London by the Pennsylvania Assembly to argue before Parliament for the good of the colony.

During all these years, as his life and work flourished, the fire of his imagination continued to burn brightly, and he fed its flame with a multitude of interests. Truly, Benjamin Franklin was interested in everything. He spoke four languages. He studied ocean currents and light waves, stovepipes and glasswork. He observed storms; he considered the mechanics of volcanoes. He immersed himself in music, playing on the violin, the harp, and the guitar.

Benjamin was never content merely to read and write about the things he studied. Always, he tinkered with them, trying to understand with both mind and hands. He experimented; he constructed; he invented. Sometimes, he was playing with fire, especially when he became interested in electricity.

Picture with me a dark rainstorm, hovering over Philadelphia on a warm day in mid-June, 1752. Thunder rumbles ominously through sullen clouds, green and gray, illuminated by flashes of lightning. Then, just above our heads, we see something unexpected: a kite is flying, a cheerful shape constructed of two strips of cedar wood and a large silk handkerchief. Its long string is tugged violently to and fro by the storm's winds, and, attached to it, winking bravely in the lightning flashes, is a large metal house key. If we follow the kite string downward just a little farther, we'll find that it leads us to a man sheltering under the roof of a rickety little shed: Benjamin Franklin, conducting an experiment. Carefully, he reaches upward and nods in satisfaction as a spark leaps through the air from the key to the tip of his thumb.

Benjamin wanted to prove that lightning is nothing more or less than an enormous electrical spark. He had proposed this idea years before and suggested that it could be proven by attaching a long metal rod to a tall steeple or tower, since metal would collect any electrical charge in the air. But no building in Philadelphia was tall enough, and the experiment lingered in the back of Benjamin's mind until he was suddenly struck with the wonderful idea to carry a metal key high aloft on the string of a kite. When the spark leaped from the key, he knew that his experiment was a success: thunderstorms were indeed generating electricity in the air. Several months later, he described the experiment in his newspaper, but, with typical humility, he did not reveal that he was the one who had completed it.

Benjamin Franklin always, first and foremost, sought to serve others. His studies and experiments were never for his own interest alone. When he studied ocean currents, he used his knowledge to create a new and better chart for sailors to use. When he studied light and heat, he invented a more efficient kind of wood stove. When he studied glass, he invented a better type of spectacles with a lens called a bifocal for seeing clearly both near and far away. And, after the kite experiment, he drew up plans for a lightning rod—a thin metal pole attached to a building's roof to collect the electrical charge and carry it harmlessly down to the ground.

In his print shop, at the meeting in Albany, on the streets of London, under a thunderous sky—wherever he was, Benjamin Franklin was learning, observing, and serving the people around him. And the days were coming, very soon, when he would be called upon to do his very greatest work: guard and guide the fragile flame of freedom as the English colonies became the United States.

We will see him at that great task in the chapters to come.

Chapter 19

A Tea Party in Boston
The Causes of Revolution

H ave you ever watched a pot of water on the stove? The glowing burner underneath is doing its work, but for many minutes the water remains quiet and still. Then, slowly, a few tiny bubbles appear at the bottom of the pot; as the heat increases, the bubbles grow larger, until, suddenly, the water is boiling in a furious dance. If the heat is high enough, the bubbles might even splash over the edge, escaping the pot entirely.

In the years after the French and Indian War, the relationship between England and its American colonies was exactly like that pot of water on a stove. England was turning up the heat, and the colonists' anger was simmering, growing ever closer to boiling over.

The problem, at first, was money, as it so often is. If the French and Indian War had cost the colonists a terrible price in pain and fear, it had also cost England a great deal of time and effort, and, most of all, money. The long wars with France and Spain had almost completely emptied England's treasury, and now, with a peace treaty signed and vast new territories to rule, England's king and Parliament began looking for ways to fill that treasury back up. Naturally, they assumed, since much of the war had been fought in the colonies, the colonists should help pay for it. The colonists might have agreed if they had been asked, but England did not ask. She simply began to take.

First, the English began to strictly enforce the Navigation Acts, which you might remember from Chapter 14. The Navigation Acts required the colonists to purchase manufactured trade goods—tools, machines, cloth, paint—from England rather than simply setting up shop and making their own. England also forbade them from trading with other countries, such as the Netherlands or Spain. As you can imagine, many colonists had chosen for years to simply ignore the Navigation Acts; a lively trade in smuggling—bringing illegal trade goods into a country without paying taxes—had developed. Now, though, the Royal Navy was patrolling the shores looking for smugglers, and English troops were searching people's barns and shops for smuggled items. The colonists began to look with suspicion upon the army of soldiers that the king had left behind in America after the French and Indian War. Why were they there? The war was over; Pontiac's rebellion had been subdued. Were those soldiers there to protect the colonists or to control them?

Then, in 1764, England's Parliament passed a law called the Sugar Act, which established *duties*—a kind of tax that must be paid by the purchaser on trade goods that come into one country from another—on things like sugar, cotton cloth, coffee, and wine—things that the colonists used every day. In 1765 came the Stamp Act. This law required that any kind of printed paper must be stamped, for a fee, by a government official. Without the stamp, no newspaper could be published, no marriage license issued, no court documents filed. Even playing cards could not be used without being stamped.

And, since that still didn't seem like enough, two days later, Parliament passed yet another tax law. This one was called the Quartering Act, and it decreed that the colonists must provide those English soldiers in their midst with shelter and food.

All of these new taxes, of course, turned up the heat under the pot and sent the colonies into an uproar. Anger boiled over in public meetings and private dinners, at picnics and parades, in taverns and in churches. In Boston, a group of men calling themselves Sons of Liberty began to meet underneath a tall elm called the Liberty Tree, planning for ways to disrupt the tax collectors and stop their work. In just a few months, there were Sons of Liberty in towns and cities across the colonies. In Virginia's colonial assembly, a young man named Patrick Henry argued against the Stamp Act so forcefully that some in the room began to shout, "Treason! Treason!" accusing him of the ultimate disloyalty to the king. But others agreed with what Patrick Henry was saying: in England, citizens could be taxed only by the lawmakers in Parliament who represented their particular parts of the country. But the colonies had no representatives in Parliament, and therefore Parliament had no right to tax them. "No taxation without representation!" This was Patrick Henry's rallying cry, and soon it was heard throughout the colonies.

In Massachusetts, a lawyer named James Otis urged that same cry. He proposed a meeting of representatives from all of the colonies to discuss their disgust with these new taxes and to write a response to send to King George and his Parliament. In October of 1765, representatives from 9 of the 13 colonies gathered in New York City. This meeting was called the Stamp Act Congress, an important name, because a *congress,* especially in those days, meant gathering *delegates* from separate, independent states to work on a common problem. As they had at Albany in 1754, the colonies were beginning to unite. Under the leadership of John Dickinson of Pennsylvania, the delegates at the Stamp Act Congress wrote a long letter to the king, which they called a "Declaration of Rights and Grievances." You have no right to tax us like this, it said, because we are not represented in Parliament. "No taxation without representation!"

In England, some angry members of Parliament sent for Benjamin Franklin who, you might remember, had been sent to London by the Pennsylvania Assembly and was still living there, working for the good of the colonies. Now Parliament demanded answers from him. Will the colonists ever pay these taxes? What would happen if we sent our soldiers and forced them to pay? Benjamin answered them wisely and firmly: if you try that, he said, you will end up with a full-blown war. Don't do it.

So, reluctantly, Britain's Parliament *repealed*—did away with—the stamp tax, hoping that this would calm the colonists' boiling anger. And yet, at the same time, they issued another decree to the colonies: the Declaratory Act, which stated that the king's authority in the colonies was absolute and that Parliament could make any law it wanted "in all cases whatsoever," to which the colonists were obliged to submit. Thus, the pot continued to simmer; no one had really moved it off the burner.

Then, in 1767, Parliament passed a new set of laws called the Townshend Acts after the man who proposed them, Charles Townshend. He had no sympathy for the colonies; in fact, he wanted to punish them for their disobedience. The Townshend Acts demanded more duties on important and necessary things like glass, lead, paints, paper, and tea. The Acts also set up a set of law courts to bring smugglers to trial. Worst of all, from the colonists' point of view, the Townshend Acts sought to make an example of the colony of New York. The colonial assembly there had refused to comply with the Quartering Act, insisting that they would not provide beds or food for the king's soldiers. To punish them for this resistance, the Townshend Acts suspended the assembly; this meant that the colonial government was not allowed to meet together or make any decisions.

The Townshend Acts frightened the colonies. It seemed as if their king and Parliament, back in England, were treating them like conquered enemies rather than loyal subjects. Across the colonies, protests arose. The colonists banded together and vowed to *boycott*—refuse to buy—any of the taxed British goods, even if that meant going without a hot cup of tea. John Dickinson of Pennsylvania took to his pen and wrote a series of 12 letters pleading the colonists' point of view, which were published in all the colonial newspapers. The suspension of the New York Assembly was an attack on all of the colonies, he argued. It was a "stroke . . . at the liberty of all . . . for the cause of *one* is the cause of *all*." What's more, he thundered, "Those who are taxed without their own consent . . . are slaves!"

In 1770 a new prime minister came to power in London, a man called Lord North. He immediately removed the duties proscribed by the Townshend Acts, all of them except for one. The colonists, he insisted, must still pay a duty on tea.

Tea. A humble, simple thing that could be found in every house. Surely the colonists wouldn't mind paying a tiny, insignificant tax on their morning cup of tea? But they did mind. It wasn't the amount of the tax or that the tax was laid on something they used every day. It was the fact that the tax existed at all.

In Boston, a man named Sam Adams wrote an article in the newspaper asking "the people of this country explicitly to declare whether they will be freemen or slaves." He called on the colonists to boycott tea and drink something else, anything else, instead. He formed a Committee of Correspondence in Boston to keep track of the colonists' complaints against the English and urged all the other colonies to do the same.

Meanwhile, in London, Lord North had instructed the English East India Company to ship thousands of pounds of tea to the colonies. The Committee of Correspondence alerted the colonists; large public protests against the hated taxes erupted. In fear of the crowds, some royal governors turned the tea ships away and sent them back to England. In South Carolina, American merchants accepted the tea and then locked it up in warehouses rather than selling it. In other colonial ports, the tea-bearing ships were not allowed to offload their cargo. Thus it was that, in December of 1773, three East India Company ships lay at anchor in Boston Harbor, hulls filled to the brim with tea.

On December 16, a group of men swarmed aboard the ships. At first glance, they looked a bit like Native Americans, with feathers and shell beads in their hair and tomahawks in their hands. But they were actually Boston's Sons of Liberty, Sam Adams at their head, and their mission was clear: no taxed tea in Boston! To the cheers of the crowd watching on shore, they chopped open the chests of tea and threw them overboard—342 chests in all. All of Boston Harbor was an enormous tea pot; by the next morning, heaps of damp, salty tea were strewn along the shoreline.

In England, news of this "tea party" was met with anger and disbelief. These Bostonians were dangerous! They might inspire more of the colonies to act in the same rebellious way. They must be dealt with at once, firmly and decisively, lest the rebellion against their mother country grow and spread. As King George wrote to Lord North, "The colonists must either submit or triumph."

And, in saying that, he was exactly right, as we will see in the chapters to come.

Chapter 20

On Lexington Green

The Shot Heard 'Round the World

Lord North, the British prime minister and leader of Parliament, moved quickly to enact several new laws, all aimed at punishing Boston for its merry tea party. One law closed Boston's port so that no ship could enter or leave and declared that it would stay closed until the Bostonians repaid Britain for all of that ruined tea. Another decreed that all of Massachusetts's governors and officials, who formerly had been elected to their offices by the colonists themselves, were now to be appointed by King George. A third law extended the hated Quartering Act, insisting that the people of Boston allow the king's soldiers to live in their houses and eat their food. And then the colonial governor of Massachusetts was replaced by a British army general named Thomas Gage.

Lord North called these laws the Coercive Acts, because his intent was to coerce the colonists to do what he wanted. But colonists all across America at once began to call the laws the "Intolerable Acts," for they were, indeed, not going to be tolerated. If the colonists did not resist, these same harsh measures might eventually be applied to all of the other colonies. They well understood that these laws were not just about Boston; they were Parliament's way of declaring its absolute authority.

The colonies hurried to support Boston. Some sent supplies; several nearby towns offered their harbors to Boston's ships. In Virginia, a young man named Thomas Jefferson stood up in Virginia's colonial assembly and proposed that they set aside a date for Virginians to earnestly pray for Boston. The English royal governor, sitting in charge of the assembly, flew into a rage and told them all to go home and never come back; the assembly was no more. Instead, the Virginian assemblymen all made their way to a nearby tavern. There, they decided to invite all of the colonies to send representatives to a Continental Congress where they could decide together how the colonies could best respond to the Intolerable Acts. The Congress would be held in Pennsylvania in the fall.

So it was that in September of 1774, 56 men made their way to Philadelphia. They were chosen to attend by the people of 12 colonies; Georgia, whose colonists were still loyal to the king, was the only colony that did not send anyone. Among these elected representatives were Sam Adams of Boston with his brother John, a wise and thoughtful lawyer; the young lawyer Patrick Henry along with his fellow Virginian, George Washington; and even Benjamin Franklin of Pennsylvania, who had journeyed home from London to be there. Together, they proposed to send to the king a Declaration of Rights written by John Adams. It strongly declared that, while England had every right to make laws concerning English ships and English trade, it had no right to interfere with the colonies' affairs. The colonists would defend themselves with their own militias and elect their own leaders and tax their own people. What's more, until the Intolerable Acts were repealed, the colonists would buy no English goods in America, and they would sell no American goods to England.

The Congressmen then turned their attention to Boston. They knew that General Gage, Boston's new governor, had asked the king and Parliament to send him 20 thousand soldiers. In the meantime, he had taken the soldiers he had and had created a fortified wall across the Boston Neck, an isthmus of land that connected the city of Boston with the rest of Massachusetts. Gage's soldiers now manned the Neck, keeping close watch upon anyone going in or out of the city. All of this sounded ominous indeed, and the men of the Continental Congress solemnly warned that if Gage attempted to rule Boston and thus Massachusetts, by force, all of the other colonies would come to its defense. Grimly, the Congressmen sent out messages, urging the colonies to alert their militias and begin gathering guns and bullets in case they might be needed.

With these decisions made, the Congressmen ended their meeting and returned to their homes, no doubt to face the questions and fears of their fellow colonists. Most colonists still called themselves Englishmen, and the idea of armed rebellion against their king and country seemed almost unthinkable.

When Patrick Henry returned home to Virginia, he found that his fellow assemblymen were reluctant to call Virginia's militia to action. Many there were unsure of taking such a step, as it would mean that war with England was certainly coming. We must continue to seek peace, they said. We must! But Patrick Henry shouted, "There is no peace. . . . What is it that gentlemen wish? What would they have? Is life so dear, or peace so sweet, as to be purchased at the price of chains and slavery? Forbid it, Almighty God! I know not what course others may take; but as for me, give me liberty or give me death!"

Thousands of his fellow colonists agreed with him. The time for talking of peace had ended; the only hope for true freedom was to fight for it. The colonial militias began to train in earnest; they came to be called "minutemen," because they could spring into action so quickly, at a minute's notice.

In London, the king's anger grew. "The New England Governments are in a state of rebellion," he said to Lord North. "Blows must decide whether they are to be subject to this country or independent." The English were confident that the colonists' rebellious fever would soon fade in the face of England's military might. One English soldier, Major John Pitcairn, wrote home declaring just that: "I am satisfied that one active campaign, a smart action, and burning two or three of their towns, will set everything to rights."

The king demanded stern action. On April 14, 1775, General Gage received a secret letter from London ordering him to do something about the rebels in Massachusetts. General Gage had learned of a militia storehouse full of guns in the village of Concord, about 18 miles from Boston. He decided to march his soldiers there and seize it, destroying all the weapons. Surely that would put a damper on these fiery rebels!

The general tried to conceal his actions, but Boston was not an easy place to keep secrets. It was full of Gage's soldiers, yes, but it was also filled with colonial spies. The Sons of Liberty were hard at work in the city, and, ever alert, some of them heard rumors of General Gage's plans. They knew that, very soon, a large party of redcoats would slip out of the city and march toward Concord. There were other, darker rumors that General Gage planned to arrest Sam Adams and John Hancock, another colonial leader, and send them off to London to be put on trial for treason.

On the evening of April 18, moving with utmost quiet under the dark night sky, 750 British soldiers climbed into boats and sailed out across the Charles River, ready to march toward the weapons storehouse in Concord as soon as they reached the opposite shore. They did not know they were being watched, and they did not notice, twinkling high in the steeple of a nearby church, two glowing lanterns.

The lanterns were a signal, devised days before by a man named Paul Revere. The Sons of Liberty in Boston could not be sure by what route the soldiers would leave the city; they might march out through the fortified gate at Boston Neck, or they might take a shortcut by sailing across the harbor in boats. So Paul Revere instructed the pastor of the church to hang signal lanterns in the steeple: "one if by land, and two if by sea," and then the people of Charlestown on the opposite shore would know where the British were moving, and they could sound the alarm.

The signal sent, Paul Revere leapt on his horse and rode toward Concord, spreading the warning as he went. The redcoats were marching! He alerted every man in every house along the way, and many of them set out on horseback, alerting every militia man they could find: *The English are marching toward Concord!* By midnight, Paul Revere had ridden 10 miles and reached the village of Lexington, where Sam Adams and John Hancock were staying, and warned them to flee.

By dawn the next morning, an advance party of 238 English soldiers had reached Lexington. They were led by Major John Pitcairn, that same Pitcairn who had written home so dismissively of the Americans' taste for rebellion. Now, as he rode into the green square in the center of the town, he saw stretched across it a line of 70 Massachusetts minutemen, silent and grim in the early morning light.

"Disperse, ye rebels, disperse!" he shouted at them. "Throw down your arms, ye villains, ye Rebels!"

In the tense silence that followed, the minutemen stood firm. Their leader, Captain John Parker, had told them, "Don't fire unless fired upon, but if they want to have a war,—let it begin here."

And then someone—to this day no one knows who—fired a shot.

At once, the redcoats shouldered their rifles and fired a volley of bullets into the line of minutemen. Eighteen men fell, eight of them mortally wounded. The minutemen retreated, and the British marched on toward Concord, only to find that, by now, the colonists had carried off and re-hidden all of the valuable weapons. Their mission failed, the redcoats turned to make the march back to Boston, 18 weary miles away.

But by now it was noon, and the countryside was alive with colonial militiamen. They were everywhere, firing their rifles from behind trees and barns, stone walls and farmhouses, all along the road that the English soldiers had to follow back to Boston. By nightfall, when the soldiers finally made it back to the city, more than 250 of them had been killed or wounded. The redcoats had paid a terrible price for the minutemen who fell on Lexington Green.

Earlier that day, hearing the sounds of gunfire, Sam Adams had exclaimed, "What a glorious morning is this!" But the Americans had paid a price too: 93 of them had fallen. As George Washington would later write in his diary about this day: "The first blood in the dispute with Great Britain was drawn."

It was the first, but not the last; much more would be spilled. The American War for Independence had begun, and six long years of struggle, defeat, and triumph were to come.

All of it began that day on Lexington Green with one single gunshot.

Years later, a beloved American poet named Ralph Waldo Emerson would remember that momentous day with a poem called Concord Hymn. It begins like this:

> *By the rude bridge that arched the flood,*
> *Their flag to April's breeze unfurled,*
> *Here once the embattled farmers stood,*
> *And fired the shot heard round the world.*

Monument at Lexington Green, Massachusetts

Chapter 21

The Spirit of 1776

The Declaration of Independence

With the shot fired at Lexington Green in April of 1775—"the shot heard 'round the world"—the American colonies were now at war with England.

After the events of that day, General Gage's soldiers retreated back to Boston, losing a large number of their company to colonial rifle shots, as we saw in the last chapter. But Boston proved to be a trap rather than a safe haven, for the Massachusetts militiamen immediately gathered and surrounded the city. By early May, they had been joined by militias from New Hampshire, Connecticut, and Rhode Island—totaling so many men that they were rapidly becoming an army. Alarmed, General Gage sent for reinforcements; he was joined by three more English generals: William Howe, Henry Clinton, and John Burgoyne, all of them experienced military leaders.

The city of Boston, set as it was on a peninsula, was protected on three sides by water. But the Charles River on Boston's northern edge was overlooked by another peninsula, itself surmounted by two large hills, Breed's Hill and Bunker Hill. From their summits, a man could easily look down into the very center of Boston. Studying this situation, General Clinton decided that his soldiers must climb and secure those hills in order to safeguard the city. He planned to send his men out on this mission on June 18.

But, hearing rumors of this scheme, the colonists formed a strategy to beat him at his own game. On the evening of June 16, with Colonel William Prescott in the lead, a force of 1,200 colonial militiamen crept through the darkness and made their way up Breed's Hill. There, moving as stealthily as they could, they worked through the night to build an earthen wall along the hill's crest. At dawn the next day, the English could see, to their dismay, that the Americans were entrenched atop the hill.

Henry Clinton and the other generals were determined to root them out. The sun was already well risen on what would prove to be a blisteringly hot day as the redcoats lined up in orderly rows and began their march up the hill.

The militiamen were waiting for them. They had been busily reinforcing their dirt wall with fence rails and bales of hay, and they crouched behind it, rifles aimed down the hill at the steadily advancing troops. Colonel Prescott warned them, "Wait until you see the white of their eyes." So they waited and waited, and the English soldiers climbed closer and closer, until, when they were only 15 strides away, the colonists let fly with a volley of rifle fire.

The redcoats fell in droves, "as thick as sheep in a fold." Those who had survived turned and fled as the militiamen cheered, hardly able to believe that they had triumphed so easily over England's military might. But the English were not defeated; they reformed their companies at the bottom of the hill and attacked once more. Again they were met with a hail of bullets; again they retreated, regrouped, and marched upward in a third attack. By this time, the colonists had begun to run out of ammunition, and many of them were forced to throw down their rifles, seize stones from the ground, and fling those down upon the enemy. But stones are not so deadly a force as bullets, and the redcoats, pressing forward, gained the top of the hill. With no other option and no more ammunition, Colonel Prescott ordered a retreat; the militiamen abandoned the hill they had so recently controlled.

A defeat? Perhaps. The Americans had no choice but to flee, and they lost 400 men. But the English losses were much greater: more than a thousand redcoats killed or wounded, including many of their officers. Surveying the damage, General Clinton said sadly that it was "a dearly-bought victory. Another such would have ruined us."

Meanwhile, down in Philadelphia, a Second Continental Congress had gathered with many of the same representatives who had attended the first. As before, they had no legal authority in the eyes of King George and Parliament, but for the Americans who were already committed to the cause of independence, the Continental Congress was the only government available. The events at Lexington and Concord had convinced the Congressmen, even those who still talked of peace and renewed friendship with England, that they must raise an army and prepare for war. Since there were already hundreds of militiamen surrounding Boston, they decided to choose a commander and send him there. But who to choose? John Adams rose to his feet with a suggestion. The obvious choice, he said, is George Washington of Virginia whose "skill and experience as an officer, . . . whose independent fortune, great talents and excellent universal good character, would command the approbation of all America."

George Washington, surprised and abashed, quickly stood and left the room to allow his fellow congressmen to vote freely. And freely they did, with not one dissenting vote. On Friday, June 15, 1775, the leader of Congress, John Hancock, officially announced that George Washington had been made "General and Commander in Chief of the Army of the United Colonies." Accepting the great task, Washington was humble and somber.

"I am truly sensible of the high honor done me," he said, "yet I feel great distress, from a consciousness that my abilities and military experience may not be equal to the extensive and important trust: However, as the Congress desire it I will enter upon the momentous duty, and exert every power I possess in their service and for the support of the glorious cause."

Immediately, he made plans to set out for Boston to take charge of the American militiamen there, who were that very day staring down at the British redcoats as they marched up Breed's Hill. They did not know, as they faced that fearsome challenge, that they were militiamen no longer; they were now the Continental Army. Once they had been ordinary citizens— farmers and shopkeepers, blacksmiths and shoemakers; now they were George Washington's soldiers.

The Continental Congress had set war in motion by commissioning George Washington and sending him to Boston, but they were by no means certain that they were doing the right thing. It is difficult and painful for people to give up on loyalties that have long been part of their lives, and such was the case with the American colonists and their mother country. For some, shedding their loyalty to King George was as simple as shrugging off an old coat; for others, their devotion and trust in England remained. Because of this, they were called loyalists, and they viewed the actions of the Continental Congress with deepening fear and dismay. How could they possibly agree with this rebellion against their king?

In Pennsylvania, a man named Thomas Paine attempted to answer that question. In early January of 1776, he wrote a *pamphlet*—an essay published like a magazine or miniature book—called *Common Sense* in which he laid the blame for all the current troubles squarely at the king's feet. The colonists rightly loved their mother country, he said, but that mother had betrayed them. The king was a "royal brute"—a vicious animal—willing to sacrifice them for his own gain. Thus,

Paine told his readers, the colonies had no choice but to seek their independence; indeed, "the cause of America is in a great measure the cause of all mankind." Paine said that all men wish to be free; he argued that the Americans now had a chance to make that dream come true.

Common Sense was uncommonly successful—150,000 copies were printed; it spread throughout the colonies and persuaded many to reconsider their opinions and shed their loyalist coats.

Thomas Paine's Common Sense

Thus it was that, on June 7 of 1776, Richard Henry Lee of Virginia stood before his fellow Congressmen and insisted that the colonies "are and of right ought to be free and independent states." John Adams stood and offered his formal agreement, and much discussion began. Thomas Jefferson of Virginia explained it like this: "The question was not whether, by a declaration of independence, we should make ourselves what we are not, but whether we should declare a fact which already exists."

A declaration is a formal announcement, a strong and resolute statement of a fact. By writing out a declaration of independence, the colonists would be telling King George and Parliament, and the whole world, that they would be England's subjects no more. They were their own people, their own government, and their own nation. They knew that once such a statement was made, it could not be unmade except by force. If England wanted the Americans to take back their declaration, they would have to conquer them in battle and force them to submit, once again, to the king.

Congress assigned Thomas Jefferson and John Adams the task of actually writing out this all-important declaration. But, knowing that Jefferson was a gifted writer, John Adams gave the job fully over to him. All through the latter half of June, Jefferson labored, spelling out the ideas that Congress had been debating, showing them what he had written, and then taking their suggestions for improvements and writing some more. It was finished and passed on July 4, 1776, and signed by the Congress president John Hancock and all 55 of the other Congressional representatives.

This is what it said in its famous opening:

"We hold these truths to be self-evident, that all men are created equal, that they are endowed by their Creator with certain unalienable Rights, that among these are Life, Liberty and the pursuit of Happiness.—That—to secure these rights, Governments are instituted among Men, deriving their just powers from the consent of the governed,—That whenever any Form of Government becomes destructive of these ends, it is the Right of the People to alter or to abolish it, and to institute new Government, laying its foundation on such principles and organizing its powers in such form, as to them shall seem most likely to effect their Safety and Happiness."

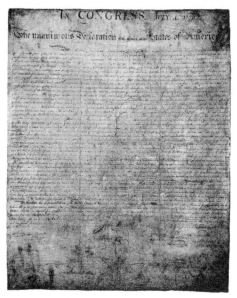

The Declaration of Independence

Colonists no longer; no longer servants of the king. Governments have their power through the consent of the governed, and the Americans no longer consented. They were now, as Richard Henry Lee had proposed, a free and independent people, the people of the United States of America.

Chapter 22

Through the Valley of the Shadow
The War for Independence

The Continental Congress had declared America's independence. Now George Washington and the Continental Army faced the task of winning it on the battlefield. And an enormous task it was, for the English army was well-trained and well-supplied, with experienced commanders and smartly-uniformed troops. The Continental Army had none of those things. It seemed hopelessly overmatched. And, indeed, during the six long years of the war, the Continental Army spent most of its time in retreat, fleeing from the enemy. It was a tiny David confronting a brawny Goliath.

But it was a David fighting on his home ground, fighting for his freedom; and that spirit, eventually, would make all the difference. The Continental Army lost most of the battles, but, ultimately, it won the war.

This is how it happened:

Having been commissioned as commander over the Continental Army in June of 1775, George Washington made his way at once to Boston where all the militiamen had surrounded the city, as we have seen. Over the next few months, as summer fled and winter crept in, he worked to bring the various militia units together into one, whole army. The English, meanwhile, were firmly planted in the city, and it seemed impossible to pry them out. But in February of that winter, Henry Knox, a young bookseller who also happened to be a weapons expert, arrived in the hills above the city with 60 heavy iron cannons, English weapons that had been captured by the Vermont militia at Fort Ticonderoga in New York. During one long night, March 5, 1776, Washington's men hauled the cannons up onto the heights around the city, and, when morning came, the redcoats found themselves—and more importantly all of their ships in the harbor—within range of deadly cannon fire. Inside the city, General Howe realized that he was bested, and he sent a messenger to Washington, proposing a deal: if Washington would allow Howe and his troops to sail away in safety, he would not burn and loot the city as they left.

Washington agreed. On March 17, thousands of English troops abandoned Boston, filing aboard 125 ships and sailing away to the north, where they would eventually disembark in Halifax, Nova Scotia. With Boston freed, Washington took the Continental Army on the march southward, toward New York.

Howe, who had been humbled but certainly not defeated by the retreat from Boston, regrouped his soldiers in Halifax and then set sail again. He, too, was aiming for New York, which he planned to capture at any cost and then use it to separate New England from the colonies in the south. On July 2, 1776, Howe began landing his troops on Staten Island in New York Harbor. Eventually, he would have 32,000 men, including 9,000 Hessians—German soldiers who were hired by the British as mercenaries. Washington, meanwhile, could gather only 20,000 militiamen. Nevertheless, he was able to tell them, on July 4th, 1776, that they were now free men fighting for the "free and independent states."

Despite the solemn and joyful news of the Declaration of Independence, events in New York were grim. Washington and his men had hurriedly built fortifications on Long Island, but to no avail. They were forced to retreat again and again through the final weeks of August. By September 15, General Howe was in complete control of New York City; he had killed or captured thousands of Washington's men. Washington continued his retreat across the Hudson River and then west into Pennsylvania. His remaining force of 6,000 men was burdened with discouragement; how could they have ever thought that they could meet the mighty redcoats in battle and defeat them? With them marched Thomas Paine, the writer of *Common Sense*. Urging Americans to avoid despair, he wrote, "These are the times that try men's souls."

Comfortable and snug in New York City, General Howe and his men settled down for the winter, assuming that with the coming of spring they would crush this rebellion once and for all. The loyalists in New York were cheering them on, and, in London, news of Howe's victories in New York prompted parties and celebrations. Howe, no doubt, felt he had earned a comfortable winter rest. But Washington, desperate to seize the day and give his troops a victory, could not afford to wait out the winter. Instead, on Christmas night of 1776, he loaded 2,500 of his men on small, flat boats and stealthily crossed the ice-choked Delaware River. On the other side, at the town of Trenton, New Jersey, they surprised a garrison of 1,500 Hessians sleepy with wine and a heavy Christmas feast. The Americans captured 900 of them, with only six men wounded on their own side. It was a daring, unexpected victory, followed just a few days later by another at Princeton where an English general named Cornwallis attempted to strike back and instead was forced into a hasty retreat by Washington's clever attacks.

These were only two small victories, but they came at the right time, and they proved to Washington's tiny, ragged army that it could win, especially if it kept moving and avoided big battles. These victories showed the English, too, that the war might not be over by spring after all.

England had no stomach for a long war; the king wanted to end the rebellion as quickly as possible. To do this, the English generals decided to bring two different armies down from their fortresses in Canada to meet at the town of Albany in New York and secure all of New York for England. Meanwhile, another army, marching from New York City under General Howe, would advance upon the city of Philadelphia.

On July 6, 1777, one of these armies, led by Major General John Burgoyne, recaptured Fort Ticonderoga. It had been held by the Continental Army ever since Henry Knox had departed with his 60 iron cannons in tow just over two years earlier.

Fort Ticonderoga

Forced to surrender the fort, the Continental Army's spirit remained strong, and as they retreated, they destroyed bridges, blocked roads, burned fields, and scraped the countryside clean of anything edible. Burgoyne, marching toward Albany, was slowed and hampered, his troops growing steadily more hungry.

Then, 15 miles short of his goal, he found himself surrounded by American forces, both militiamen and the Continental Army, led by American generals Horatio Gates and Benedict Arnold, and they were reinforced by more soldiers hastily sent north by George Washington. Over the course of a week or so in mid-September, Burgoyne twice tried to fight his way through the American lines to gain the safety of Albany; both attempts failed. They were sharp, fierce battles, but the Americans held firm, and when the gunsmoke had cleared and night fell, Burgoyne found that he had lost more than a thousand men. Worried now, and knowing himself to be outnumbered, he gathered his men and retreated into the darkness, marching all night until they came to a town called Saratoga.

But the Americans followed him there and surrounded him once more. With no hope of victory and no sign of any reinforcements from the other English commanders, Burgoyne gave up. He surrendered his entire army of 6,000 men and sailed back to England, never to fight another battle.

The English had always considered their army to be vastly superior to the American force. Their strategy, from the very beginning, was to end the war quickly by forcing Washington and the Continental Army into an enormous battle and crushing them out of existence. But the American victory at Saratoga gave them pause. One English officer said, "The courage and obstinacy with which the Americans fought were the astonishment of everyone and we now became fully convinced that they are not that contemptible enemy we had hitherto imagined them." George Washington would have agreed with those thoughts. He knew his men; he valued their courage, and he knew that they alone kept the "Glorious Cause" alive. And, despite the victory at Saratoga, that courage and that cause were about to face a terrible test.

For you see, while Burgoyne was running into trouble in New York, General Howe had marched his army toward Philadelphia. He forced Washington to retreat at the Battle of Brandywine Creek on September 11, 1777, and captured

Philadelphia just two weeks later. Or perhaps, as Benjamin Franklin put it, Philadelphia captured him. The city's warm homes and many comforts proved an irresistible temptation, and Howe settled down with his army to wait out the winter. George Washington encamped for the winter as well, just 20 miles away in Valley Forge, Pennsylvania, where both comfort and warmth were in very short supply.

It was a dreadful season for Washington and his men, truly "a valley of the shadow of death." Bitterly cold, they shivered in rude wooden huts, lacking blankets, firewood, food, coats, and even shoes. Hundreds of men fell ill; by winter's end Washington had lost 2,000 of them. Some men, desperate and despairing, drifted away, abandoning Washington and the Army, certain the cause was lost.

But many more stayed, enduring the weeks of cold and sorrow. And Washington knew, as he suffered with them, that the longer they stayed together, the longer they endured, the stronger the possibility of winning. As long as the Army was alive, so too was the Revolution.

He was right, of course, for news of the Continental Army's victory at Saratoga had reached Europe, where it lodged thoughtfully in the minds of the leaders of France. They were England's enemies of old, as we have seen; now, sensing the turning of the tide, they agreed to meet with American *diplomats* led by our old friend Benjamin Franklin. On February 6, 1778, the French and the Americans signed a treaty of alliance, pledging to help one another and not to lay down their weapons until England had acknowledged American independence. Over the next few months, France sent 12 warships to help guard the coast and fight off the Royal Navy, as well as experienced officers to help guide the troops. One of these was Gilbert du Motier, Marquis de Lafayette (jheelbair duh mo-TYAY mar-KEE deh LAUGH-aye-eht), who became an enormous admirer and follower of George Washington.

With the French entering the war, the English generals fixed upon a new strategy: they would gather all of their troops back in New York, which was still soundly in their hands, and then focus all of their attention on the southern colonies. At first, this change in plans seemed to be working: the redcoats captured the city of Savannah, Georgia, in December of 1778 and then Charleston, South Carolina in 1780. The English General Cornwallis inflicted a disastrous defeat on the Continental Army at Camden, South Carolina, where the American troops broke and ran in terror from the battlefield. Woe followed woe then, for General Benedict Arnold, so brave at Saratoga, turned traitor. He agreed to turn over West Point, the fort that he commanded, to the English, and it was soon discovered that he had been spying for them and against George Washington for more than a year. To Washington's grave sorrow, Benedict Arnold joined Cornwallis, who had marched his army up from South Carolina into Virginia, where he encamped at a place called Yorktown. Cornwallis expected to receive reinforcements from General Clinton in New York.

Washington sent Lafayette after Cornwallis with 4,000 men. Then, to keep Clinton locked away, he wrote letters describing a plan to attack New York and plotted to let them fall, seemingly by accident, into English hands. As he had hoped, Clinton and all his troops stayed safely entrenched in New York, watching anxiously for Washington to arrive. But meanwhile, the General and all the rest of the Continental Army were marching northward to Virginia.

And so it was that, in October of 1781, General Cornwallis found himself besieged with Lafayette and Washington surrounding him. He might have fled to sea, but the French navy appeared, blockading the shore and preventing any escape. After one unsuccessful attempt to break free, Cornwallis surrendered to Washington on October 19. Humiliated and exhausted, he refused to appear personally; he sent an underling to present Washington with his captured sword.

The next day, a Sunday, the members of the Continental Congress walked together to church, there to thank God for the "victory of a great and good man in a great and good cause."

And, several weeks later, when the news of the surrender at Yorktown reached England, Lord North groaned, "It is all over!"

It was. Though British troops lingered in America for another year or more, the fighting had ended. In 1782, King George announced that he would formally recognize his former colonies as free and independent states, and, on September 3, 1783, once more under the leadership of Benjamin Franklin, a treaty to end the war was signed in Paris. From Maine to Georgia and westward to the Mississippi River, the land that had once been England's 13 colonies was England's no longer. The Americans had won their war for independence; the country was theirs—to do with as they wished.

George Washington

Chapter 23

We the People

The Constitution of the United States

B ut now what?

The people of the new United States were no longer ruled by a king. They were no longer tied to England or to any part of the Old World. Yet, they must have some sort of government, because any group of people living in the same land must have a way to make laws and judge wrongdoers, to defend against enemies, and to build roads and bridges and ports. Their old government lay dismantled before them, like the heaps of wood and canvas and iron that remain after a ship has run aground and wrecked itself upon a strange shore. If the people were to sail safely once more, they must build a new ship.

They remembered, of course, what a government looked and felt like when they were ruled by England. They knew the basic shape that the ship must take in order to float. They could study, too, the patterns of those who had gone before, the governments of the ancient world; they could read the wisdom of the Bible and of philosophers as they discussed what a nation should be. But, ultimately, with England's surrender at Yorktown, they were on their own. They had fought for their liberty and won it. Now they must turn away from making war and find a way to make a nation.

During the first few years of the War for Independence, the Continental Congress had run things: they had raised the Continental Army, put George Washington in charge of it, paid the soldiers, and negotiated the alliance with France. But when the Declaration of Independence was signed in 1776, the members of the Continental Congress knew that something more solid and official must be put into place. So they wrote a plan called the Articles of Confederation, which officially created the United States of America. The Articles organized a new Congress, the Confederation Congress, in which each of the 13 states had a single vote. This Congress took care of the things that affected the United States as a whole: it could judge quarrels between states; it was in charge of the postal service and the *mint*—the agency that created money. It watched over the new western territories, such as Kentucky. And it could declare war and negotiate peace treaties, which is exactly what it was doing when it sent Benjamin Franklin to shepherd the Treaty of Paris in 1783. Meanwhile, each individual state would be run by its own *legislature*—a group of people who are chosen by the citizens' votes and make the laws for the state.

For a few years the Articles of Confederation sailed confidently along. But leaks soon appeared and the ship began to wobble. The Articles, you see, were not strong enough. They were like a little boat folded out of paper instead of a vessel fortified with tough wooden beams. The Articles did not provide for courts, so there was no one to administer justice and judge the laws. And they did not give the government any way to raise money, so it could not pay for the things that it was meant to administer, such as the soldiers in the Continental Army. And the Articles did not put anyone in charge; there was no actual head of government.

This might seem strange to us; why would the Articles' writers, who were all wise men and members of the Continental Congress, create a government with such weaknesses? But, you must remember that all Americans were fearful of a strong central government, because, after all, that was what they had already experienced under the rule of England. That is what they had just fought a bloody, six-year-long war to escape.

By 1785 though, most of America's leading thinkers could see that the Articles of Confederation were not working. A young lawyer from New York named Alexander Hamilton suggested that the states attempt a solution. He proposed that every state send delegates to a special *convention*—a meeting—in Philadelphia in May of 1787. There, they would devise such "provisions as shall appear to them necessary to render the constitution of the Federal Government adequate to the exigencies [needs] of the Union." In other words, he was suggesting that the Articles of Confederation be rewritten and recreated into something strong and workable: the Constitution of the United States of America.

The Constitution! Those are words that you might have heard, words with a noble ring. And noble it is, for a nation's Constitution is a mighty thing. Although in and of itself it appears to be merely a piece of parchment, a fine-looking document, it is actually so much more. A constitution sets forth the supreme rights and laws of a nation, governing all the citizens who live in it. A Constitution is what makes a nation what it is.

Thus it was that, on Sunday, May 13 of 1787, George Washington rode into Philadelphia. Bells rang to honor him; soldiers paraded along the road as he passed. But the joyous welcome masked a serious, solemn purpose; for he had come as a delegate from the Virginia legislature to the Philadelphia Convention. He had been concerned about the Articles of Confederation from the very beginning; in a letter sent to the states' legislatures, he had called it a "rope of sand" incapable of truly binding the states together. Only a strong Constitution could do that. And so he, along with 54 others, had come to Philadelphia to create one.

It was a fearsome task, but they were a remarkable group of men. They came from 12 of the 13 states—Rhode Island alone did not send any delegates. They were professional men, most of them: lawyers, merchants, bankers, planters, all widely educated in history, law, and philosophy. But they were also men of action: most of them had been part of the Continental Congress, 21 of them had fought in the War, seven of them had been state governors. Eight of them had boldly signed the Declaration of Independence, risking the wrath of King George. The oldest among them was Benjamin Franklin, who was carrying on the great work of his life even at the venerable age of 81; the most honored was George Washington, who was chosen from among them to preside over—to lead—the meetings.

They set to work in the east room of the Pennsylvania State House, in the same room where the Declaration of Independence had been signed. For the next four months, through the baking hot Philadelphia summer, they hammered out the principles of the Constitution, the beams and struts that would give shape to a new Ship of State.

The Pennsylvania State House, now called Independence Hall

In the beginning, they could only agree on certain big ideas: that government can exist only if the people consent, or agree, to be governed; that therefore people must have a voice in their government; but also that a way must be found to protect the nation as a whole from being dominated by any one group. But how to put these ideas into action, into a government that actually worked? Slowly, two different plans came into being.

The first arose in the mind and heart of James Madison of Virginia. A young man of 36, he was nonetheless a powerful scholar who had long studied the ideas of government and philosophy. His plan, which came to be called the Virginia Plan, called for a government organized into three different branches, like a thick-limbed tree. One branch would be legislative. The people in that branch would debate over and create the nation's laws as a congress divided into two groups, called houses: a lower house elected by the people of their states and an upper house of men chosen by their state governments. The second branch would be executive: these men would put the laws into practice. The third branch would be judicial: these would be the judges, who would carefully consider whether the laws that were made were in agreement with the Constitution. Every person who lived in the nation would be subject to these laws, regardless of what state he lived in.

For many days, the delegates debated over this plan. Would it work? Did it take too much power away from the states themselves? Finally, some of the delegates proposed a second plan, the New Jersey Plan, which kept the three branches but did away with the upper house in the congress and left only the lower house whose members were chosen by the votes of the people. The New Jersey Plan also gave Congress the power to *levy* taxes on the people and created a Supreme Court whose judges would have the final word on any dispute in the land.

The delegates could see virtues in both plans, but they also saw problems that sparked furious debates among them.

First, how would this legislative branch, this congress, be chosen? Should not larger states, with many more citizens, be allowed to send more representatives? Not so! cried the delegates from the smaller states; if that happens, we will always be overlooked, and none of our problems addressed. Well, then, should every state, regardless of population, send the same number of representatives to the Congress? That won't work! protested the larger states, for then the states with few people will have just as loud a voice as the states with huge cities and many citizens. That wouldn't be fair!

Over and over, round and round; the discussion went back and forth. Finally, Roger Sherman of Connecticut proposed a compromise: let the Congress be two houses, as outlined in the Virginia Plan, but let one house be a House of Representatives, where the number of each state's congressmen depends upon its population, and let the other house be a Senate, where each state, large or small, sends two men to the Congress. All agreed, and the problem was solved.

But another somber problem loomed, for the delegates from the northern states and those from the south disagreed with regard to slavery. Slaves had been brought to America from the beginning through the Triangle Trade, and by now, 150 years since the colonies were founded, the slaves and the work they did were an ever-present part of life, especially in southern colonies like Georgia and the Carolinas. If the representatives from the states were based upon the number of people living there, why then of course the southern states wanted to count the slaves. The northern states did not. Some of them had already outlawed the practice of slavery, and they insisted that the national government should do the same. But the southern delegates protested, and, finally, another compromise was reached: a slave would be counted, but only as three-fifths of a person. Neither side was completely satisfied with this, but the delegates continued onward. Nevertheless, the question of slavery was a lead weight upon the ship of state, burdening its path, and would be for many years to come until finally it would erupt into a tragic Civil War. You will learn about that as you continue to study the history of our nation.

But for now, having settled the problems of representation as best they could, the delegates set into place the way that the three branches would intertwine. The laws that would be created by the two houses of Congress would be put into action by the head of the executive branch, a leader to be called the president. The delegates decided that this person, whoever he might be, would be chosen by the people's votes and would serve in this office for four years, after which either he would be re-elected or some other person would be elected. He would have the power to deny, or veto, any law that Congress made or to approve it and put it to work by signing it. There would be a vice president, too, a second-in-command who could take over the office if the president should die or step down. The president was also given the responsibility of choosing the judges who would fill out the judicial branch of the government and make sure that the laws of the land line up truly with the Constitution's principles. Any law that they deemed unconstitutional would be struck down.

Can you see the wisdom in what these men created? Congress and the president chosen by the people, the Supreme Court chosen by the president and approved by Congress, all of them needing to work together to create and empower the laws of the land, with the Constitution as the foundation of it all. No one branch can stand alone; no one branch is stronger than the other two. Like a braided rope of three cords, the three separate branches form one whole government.

On September 17, 1787, the delegates at the Philadelphia Convention gathered in the east room of the State House one last time. There, one by one, each man signed his name on the creamy white parchment of the Constitution, the document that contained, in flowing, beautiful words, the decisions they had made and the government they had created. It begins like this:

> *We the People of the United States, in Order to form a more perfect Union, establish Justice, insure domestic Tranquility, provide for the common defense, promote the general Welfare, and secure the Blessings of Liberty to ourselves and our Posterity, do ordain and establish this Constitution for the United States of America.*

The Constitution of the United States

Of course, that isn't the end of the story. The Constitution itself stated plainly that it would only start working when the states had approved—or *ratified*—it. For many months, in every state's legislature, the Constitution was debated and considered and, finally, approved. New York City was chosen as the capital of this new government, and dates for the very first election were set. Benjamin Franklin, watching all this, wrote to a friend, "Our new Constitution is now established, everything seems to promise it will be durable; but, in this world, nothing is certain except death and taxes."

He was right, of course, as he was about so many things. It has lasted. For more than 200 years, the United States has sailed bravely forward with its Constitution as both its rudder and its sail, a "more perfect union" welded together by those 55 men in a room in Philadelphia all those years ago.

Chapter 24

Walking the Wilderness Road

Daniel Boone

I magine with me a deep forest. The sun, high above, is blazing bright, but here, under the trees' broad canopies, the cool shadows beckon as the leaves whisper secrets. A narrow trail, a suggestion of a passage, makes its way through the tree trunks. A spring drips over a nearby rock ledge and gathers into a pool at its base. There—look!—a fox creeps forward on gentle paws, dipping his black nose for a drink and startling a pink salamander. He lifts his head then, ears cocked forward, eyes wary. He hears footsteps.

A man appears, striding briskly along the trail, his eyes watchful, his shoulders thrown back, a curved hunting knife in his belt and a long rifle in his hand. He's dressed in soft deerskin, weathered and brown, and he looks as much a part of this forest as the fox who has melted away into the shadows. His name is Daniel Boone; he is an American *pioneer,* one of the very first, and this trail he walks is the Cumberland Gap in the furthest American *frontier*, gateway to the land of Ken-ta-ke.

Daniel Boone was born into frontier lands and walked them all his life. His father and mother had roots in faraway England, but they had come to America, built a one-room log cabin in the wilds of Pennsylvania, and welcomed their son, the sixth of 11 children, into the world in 1734. From his earliest years, young Daniel was a hunter and a wanderer and interested in everyone and everything. He was well acquainted with the Native Americans who lived near his home, and from them he learned to walk softly through the forest, his rifle always ready. He spent very little time in school, but his family did not seem to mind. "Let the girls do the spelling," his father once said, "and Dan will do the shooting." Daniel indeed did the shooting— he provided many needed household goods for his family by trading furs and skins for them—but he did the reading too. He always took a Bible with him when he was out wandering, and usually other books as well, and he would entertain the other hunters in the evenings by reading to them as they sat around the campfire.

Daniel's family moved to North Carolina in about 1750, where Daniel's eye was caught by a pretty neighbor, Rebecca Bryan. After a courtship of three years, they married in 1756, when Rebecca was 17. Daniel and Rebecca would raise 10 children together, and together they would venture far into the wilderness.

At first, Daniel was content to let Rebecca manage their growing family at home while he supported them all by embarking on months-long hunting trips. Often alone, deep in the forest, he would spend the quiet winters hunting deer and trapping beaver, bringing his harvest home in the spring to sell to commercial fur traders. But by the 1760s, when he and Rebecca had been married 10 years or so, he felt himself growing restless. The countryside around their cabin was filling up as more and more people came to America; he declared that he needed "elbow room." And so, he tells us, "It was the first of May, in the year 1769, that I resigned my domestic happiness for a time, and left my family and peaceable habitation on the Yadkin River, in North-Carolina, to wander through the wilderness of America, in quest of the country of Kentucke."

Kentucky! Daniel had heard tales of this fabled land, tales of rich red earth and towering trees, of soft rain and warm days, of deer and bear and fish, of rambling roses and sweet, wild berries. He knew its name: "Ken-ta-ke," from an Iroquois word which meant "meadow." He knew that this lovely place lay over the Appalachian Mountains to the west.

Armed with his long rifle, his hunting knife, and a Native war hatchet—a *tomahawk*—Daniel Boone set out on a bright morning in May, leading a party of five men. He meant to travel through a narrow valley called the Cumberland Gap following the Warrior's Path, an ancient trail that the Native people had been using for many years to travel from the Ohio Valley to their hunting grounds in the southern Appalachians. On June 7, just a few weeks later, he climbed to the top of a hill called Pilot Knob and beheld for the first time the "beautiful level of Kentucke": wide rolling plains of blue-green grass, blowing softly in the wind.

Early map of the Kentucky territory, originally part of Virginia

In 1773, Daniel and his wife, along with their children and Daniel's brother Squire, left North Carolina and made their way along the Warrior's Path toward the Cumberland Gap and the land of Kentucky. They led a group of 50 intrepid settlers, all of them bent on establishing the first American settlement west of the Appalachian Mountains. Daniel's descriptions of Kentucky's beauty had fired their hearts with eagerness and made their feet light, but soon the party found itself engulfed in sorrow and difficulty.

You see, on October 9th of that year, as they were traveling, several of the younger men—including Daniel's oldest son, James—broke away from the rest of the group and went foraging for supplies. But they were captured by Natives from the Shawnee and Cherokee tribes, and three of the young men, James Boone among them, were killed.

The Shawnee and the Cherokee had watched the coming of American settlers with great concern. Kentucky was valuable land to them; it was a fertile, abundant hunting ground. And while the Iroquios tribe, who also hunted there, had signed a treaty giving away their rights to the land, the Shawnee and the Cherokee had never done so. Now they were afraid, desperately afraid, that they were about to find their pathways blocked, their hunting grounds fenced and made into settlers' farms. And so, angry and frightened, they decided that they must send a harsh warning—and harsh it was, indeed, for the Boone family, for it cost them the life of their son.

The attack upon the young men horrified the settlers, and they abandoned their plan to make a new home in Kentucky and turned back. This was the start of a year-long struggle between the Natives and the colonists for control of Kentucky. All through the summer of 1774, Daniel journeyed hundreds and hundreds of miles, warning the colonists throughout the region that the Native tribes were preparing for war and helping to defend colonial settlements against Native attacks. In October of 1774, the Shawnees were defeated in battle by the Virginia militia and afterward agreed to cease their attacks and relinquish their claim to Kentucky. Daniel then went to the leaders of the Cherokee; he arranged a meeting in which the Cherokee sold their land in Kentucky to the colonists.

The way to Kentucky now seemed clear; Daniel and 30 other woodsmen spent the summer of 1775 widening and smoothing the narrow Warrior's Path into a broad way called the Wilderness Road. Over the next 25 years, more than 300,000 settlers would travel that road. They were mostly Scotsmen and Irishmen from Pennsylvania and Virginia; they came with just a few tools and the clothes on their backs, usually on foot, leading a mule or a cow. In the rolling Kentucky countryside, each man would find a plot of land that suited him and mark its boundary by chopping a notch into a tree. There, on these new farms, they grew beans and melons and corn; they raised pigs for meat and cows for butter and cream and taught their sons and daughters the ways of the frontier.

These were America's first pioneers. A pioneer is someone who ventures into the unknown to create a new home and settle new land. But, you may be thinking, surely all of the colonists were pioneers, since all of them crossed the ocean to a new land in America. And, by a strict definition of that word, you would be right. But, in America, the word *pioneer* came to have a more narrow and special meaning: it described someone who was headed west, across the mountains, into the wilderness; someone driving a wagon filled with farming tools with his family walking beside, with the civilized cities of the eastern coast far behind and America's wide plains ahead.

These were the people who walked the Wilderness Road into Kentucky. And Daniel Boone was the first of them. At the intersection of the Road and the Kentucky River, he built a town called Boonesborough. As the years went by, and Kentucky gradually filled with settlers, he was always looking to the west, to the edges of civilized land, where he could find "elbow room."

An old picture of Daniel Boone shows him at the end of his life. He is dressed in deerskin still, seated on a rock, with Kentucky's bluegrass blowing softly beside him. A rifle rests against his knee, and his hunting dog sits patiently by his side. His eyes are lifted to the horizon, into the far distance, where the frontier was always waiting.

He was a pioneer all his life. As America grew, uncounted others would follow in his footsteps, pushing the frontier ever farther to the west, toward the setting sun.

Daniel Boone

Chapter 25

The Way Forward

The First Presidents

Have you ever found yourself in a place truly dark, perhaps deep inside a cave or in a windowless hallway? Or perhaps you've played a game of Blindman's Bluff: the blindfold tied across your eyes as your friends, laughing, try to avoid your touch? In any of these cases, the way forward cannot be clearly seen, and you stretch out your hands, moving slowly, so that you don't fall. You trust the firm ground beneath you, but you slide your feet carefully, testing for obstacles that might trip you up.

In much the same way, the men who guided the United States through its first few years of life were feeling their way forward in the dark. No one had walked this path before. The Constitution was firm and solid, upholding them, but no one could foresee the obstacles that might arise. No one could predict the challenges that the new nation might face. They simply had to begin walking, one foot in front of the other, taking the best care they could to lead the people safely forward.

And so it should come as no surprise that, faced with walking into the unknown, the people of the United States chose as their leader someone they knew and loved: George Washington. Washington had shepherded them safely through the storm of war; he had presided over the birth of the Constitution. On February 4, 1789, he was elected president of the United States, the first to bear that honored title.

It was not an honor that he had sought; indeed, his dearest wish after the war had ended was to return to his home at Mount Vernon, Virginia, and settle into the busy, useful life of a gentleman farmer. But, upon receiving word that he had been elected, he squared his shoulders and made his plans to move to New York City and take up the task he'd been given. "I was summoned by my country," he would say later, "whose voice I can never hear but with veneration and love."

On April 30 of that same year, he was *inaugurated*, formally placed into an office or position. Dressed in a dark suit with silver buttons embossed with eagles, he was brought to the steps of Federal Hall in New York City in a yellow carriage drawn by six fine white horses. On the building's balcony, as the crowds watched, he placed his hand upon a Bible and promised to defend and protect the Constitution. He was the first; every president since his day has done the same. After the ceremony, Americans lined the streets and cheered "Long live George Washington, president of the United States!"

As the Constitution had declared, in 1789 the newly-elected members of the Senate and the House of Representatives assembled as the first Congress of the United States. Together with the new president, they were feeling their way forward, seeking the best path for the nation to walk.

Washington began by establishing his *cabinet*, a group of official advisors who also serve as the leaders of *executive departments*—specific parts of the executive branch headed by the president. For his first cabinet, Washington chose Thomas Jefferson to head the State Department, which would handle the United States's interactions with other nations, and Henry Knox to lead the War Department. Then, needing a man to take care of the nation's money, he put Alexander Hamilton in charge of the Treasury.

Money was a thorny issue, because each of the former colonies had been forced to borrow a great deal from other nations, especially from France and the Netherlands, in order to fight and win the war with England. Now all of that debt must be repaid, and some of the states had no way to do so. Hamilton proposed that the United States government as a whole—its federal, or central, government—should take all the states' debt onto itself and pay it. In this way, the states would be more tightly bound to each other and to the national government, and the United States would demonstrate to other nations that it was an equal and honorable partner in financial matters. Hamilton also created the First Bank of the United States, which was responsible for collecting taxes, holding the government's money, and printing paper money for everyone in the nation to use.

Meanwhile, as President Washington and his cabinet got to work, the first Congress of the United States was also finding its way forward. Their first order of business was to *amend*—or change—the Constitution.

But wait! you may be thinking. The Constitution has only just been created, and already these men are working to change it? But one of the brilliant, wonderful things about the Constitution is that its writers knew that it might need to be adjusted or changed as the nation grew, and they wrote into it a fair and just way to do so. Any proposed *amendment* to the Constitution must first be agreed upon by almost all of the Congressmen. Then it must be sent from Congress to the individual states. Only if most of them also agree to it, is the amendment made. Here, then, in its first few months of meeting, Congress began as one of its first tasks to prepare a list of amendments for the states to consider.

You see, during those months when the Constitution was being ratified, four states—Massachusetts, New York, Virginia, and North Carolina—asked Congress to add a "bill of rights" to the Constitution. A *bill* is an idea for a law written down so that it can be debated and acted upon by Congress, and a *right* is a power or privilege that is just and moral and, thus, due to every person. In both the House of Representatives and the Senate, the Congressmen considered and debated until they had produced 10 amendments protecting individual rights, such as the right to speak freely and the right to worship as one sees fit. The states agreed to them in the year 1791, and they were added to the Constitution. These 10 amendments are still called the Bill of Rights; to this day they provide personal, individual freedoms to every citizen of the United States.

The Bill of Rights was a great accomplishment, but the Congressmen did not sit back and congratulate themselves. Pressing forward with their work, they created a system of courts and judges across the 13 states; they raised money for the new nation by establishing duties on foreign trade; and they decided upon a new capital city, to be built on a 10-square-mile plot of land along the banks of the Potomac River in Virginia and to be named Washington, in honor of the much revered first president.

George Washington was president for eight years, two of the four-year terms provided by the Constitution. Many of his friends asked him to consider serving for a third term as well, but he refused. He was wary of staying too long, of seeming too much like a king, and so in 1797 John Adams was elected by the people as America's second president, and George Washington returned with joy to his beloved home at Mount Vernon. There, just two years later, he fell ill after a horseback ride on a cold December day. On December 14, 1799, he assured the family and friends gathered around his bed that he did not fear death. "'Tis well," he said, and breathed his last.

And so it was well, although the nation, and indeed the world, grieved his loss. He was, as one of his friends sadly proclaimed, "first in war, first in peace, and first in the hearts of his countrymen." George Washington had guided the United States through its first infant steps with a hand both steady and firm. Now the responsibility for that guidance would pass to other hands.

John Adams was president for four years, during which the new capital city at present-day Washington, D.C., began to rise along the Potomac's grassy banks. A house was built for the American presidents to use, a lovely mansion with tall, noble pillars along its front, painted a snowy white. John and his wife Abigail moved their belongings into the house while it was still being built. On the second day they lived there, John Adams wrote, "I pray Heaven to bestow the best of blessings on this house and all that shall hereafter inhabit it. May none but honest and wise men ever rule under this roof." He understood, you see, the great responsibility that the president cradles in his hands, the hard decisions and urgent work that must take place within the walls of the president's "White House"; even now as you sit and read this book, an American president lives and labors there, and we must hope John Adams's prayer will uphold him.

In 1801, the people of the United States elected their third president: Thomas Jefferson, the very same man who had penned the words of the Declaration of Independence. The nation was stepping forward more confidently now—Congress had authorized the formation of a navy and begun to build a fleet of warships; the Constitution was holding firm, with the government working as it should; three different men had been elected president, and, without bloodshed or turmoil, power had passed peacefully from one to the next.

Growing in stature as a nation, then, the United States also grew in size. In 1789, when Washington became president, the United States was home to 4 million people. It stretched from the Atlantic coastline to the Mississippi River. But by 1803, with Jefferson at the helm, America's borders stretched far, far to the west, across the Great Plains, all the way to the Rocky Mountains. In just 14 years, the United States had doubled in size.

How could this happen? That is the extraordinary story of the Louisiana Purchase and the journey of Meriwether Lewis and William Clark. We will meet them in the next chapter.

(left to right) Presidents George Washington, John Adams, and Thomas Jefferson

Chapter 26

Way Out West

The Lewis and Clark Expedition

On a bright August afternoon in the year 1805, deep in the wilderness that would one day be the state of Idaho, a small band of people made their way along a narrow, tumbling stream. Around them rose the majestic bulk of the Rocky Mountains, and they toiled ever upward, aiming for a ridge slung between the higher peaks. When they reached it, their leader called for a halt and stood for long minutes gazing into the land ahead where rank upon rank of mountains marched onward like the waves of a mighty granite ocean. At that moment, he had reached one of his life's greatest goals: he was standing on the Continental Divide at the very edge of the United States. Instructing his men to wait, he walked a little way down the far side of the ridge until he found a bubbling creek running out of the mountain snow. He bent down and scooped up a handful of cold, clear water and drank. How he rejoiced in it! For this was a stream that would cascade down the mountain slopes, and eventually its waters would join with many others, and far to the west it would flow out into the Pacific. In this small sip, he could taste the ocean.

His name was Captain Meriwether Lewis, and traveling with him were thirty-some other people: his co-captain, William

Clark; soldiers, woodsmen, and boatmen; a young Native American woman and her newborn son; a man who was a slave; and one man who was not American at all, but French. Bounding alongside: a large, fluffy, black dog named Seaman. How they all came to be there, voyaging through the wilderness beyond the reach of any map, is one of America's greatest adventure tales: the story of Lewis and Clark and the journey of the Corps of Discovery.

Page from the journals of the Corps of Discovery

When Thomas Jefferson became president in 1801, the western border of the United States was formed by the Mississippi River. Everything beyond that—the whole stretch of the Great Plains, all the way west to the Rocky Mountains, and south to the city of New Orleans—was controlled by France. It was called the Louisiana Territory after France's King Louis XVI. But France, having gone through her own revolution, was no longer ruled by a king; instead, its leader was a military general named Napoleon Bonaparte who had come to power in 1799 and was determined to make France into a great empire. This immense territory in North America was a part of this plan.

President Jefferson hoped otherwise. He sent diplomats to Paris to ask Napoleon to sell part of France's territory to the United States: the city of New Orleans and the west bank of the Mississippi River. But, to Jefferson's surprise, in April of 1803, Napoleon suddenly offered to sell not only New Orleans but the whole of the Louisiana Territory. He needed money, you see, for his wars in Europe, and so he decided to sacrifice any ideas about building a French stronghold in North America.

There was no time to take the issue to Congress; Napoleon might change his mind at any moment. So, using his power as president, Jefferson authorized the purchase of the Louisiana Territory for 15 million dollars.

Now, that may seem like a great deal of money, and of course it is, but consider what it bought! With the stroke of his pen, Jefferson had added 828,000 square miles of land to the United States, doubling its size. He paid only three cents for every acre of land from the Mississippi to the Rockies in the west, from the Gulf of Mexico to Canada in the north. Although Spain still controlled the southwestern corner of the continent, from Texas over to California, the Louisiana Purchase gave the United States an enormous portion of North America, most of it uncharted. It was an incredible bargain.

The Louisiana Purchase

Congress agreed. When Jefferson came to them in October of that year to request that they approve the purchase and release the money, they did so with little fuss. That same day, they also granted another of Jefferson's requests: $2,500 to fund an expedition to explore all of this new territory.

Jefferson began assembling a team of explorers, to be called the Corps of Discovery. His goals for them were many: to map the newly acquired lands, to study its plants and animals, to establish trade with the Native tribes along the way, to make the American claim to this land strong and clear, and to prevent England and Spain from crowding in. Most of all, he wanted his team to find a practical route across the continent; it was the old dream of the Northwest Passage, renewed by the reports of a giant river far to the west which emptied into the Pacific—the Columbia. Surely, Jefferson reasoned, his Corps of Discovery could find a way to connect the continent's rivers and find "the most direct and practicable water communication across this continent."

For the expedition's leader, Jefferson chose Captain Meriwether Lewis who had been his personal secretary. Lewis was an officer in the United States Army and spoke several Native languages. He was an excellent outdoorsman; nevertheless, Jefferson took great pains to prepare him fully for the great task ahead. He arranged for Lewis to study medicine and astronomy, navigation and mapmaking. Lewis learned how to describe and preserve plant and animal specimens and how to understand rocks and minerals and fossils. He traveled to Jefferson's home, a lovely mansion called Monticello, where the president had gathered an enormous library on the subject of North American geography. Lewis spent weeks there, studying the maps and books and planning the expedition.

When all was prepared, Lewis recommended William Clark—a friend who had served alongside him in the Army—as the expedition's co-leader. The two of them then chose 29 young soldiers to accompany them. They were joined by a tall, strong man named York, a slave left to William Clark as an inheritance from his father. And, as a final member, Lewis brought his dog Seaman to help guard the men from wild animals.

In the spring of 1804, the expedition left St. Louis, Missouri, in a boat that Lewis had designed, with two large canoes skimming alongside. They hoped to sail upstream on the Missouri River as far as it would take them. An army officer, seeing them off, described the scene: "All of [the boats] were deeply laden and well manned. [Lewis and] his men possess great resolution and they are in the best health and spirits." They would need them: they would not return for more than two years, and the journey ahead would last 8,000 miles.

They rowed westward through what is now Missouri, Iowa, Nebraska, and South Dakota. Tucked into the belly of their boat were boxes filled with gifts for any Native tribes they might meet: beads, cooking pots, tools, mirrors. But for the first few months, as they made their way up the Missouri River, they seldom encountered any people; most of the Natives were far from the river, hunting the bison out on the Plains. Instead they saw miles upon miles of grassland alive with birds and insects, home to endless herds of bison, elk, and antelope. They moved slowly, exploring the countryside and making maps as the summer faded away and autumn frosts began to glitter on the grass.

By December, with winter's icy grip tightening around them, they found themselves at a place called Fort Mandan in the present-day state of North Dakota. There the expedition set up a camp to wait out the snow and ice. As they settled in, many of the Natives living nearby came to visit, intrigued by Lewis and Clark's mission and in the possibilities for trade. Communication was difficult, at first, until Lewis discovered that among the Natives was a French fur trapper named Toussaint Charbonneau who was willing to serve as an interpreter. When the winter ended and the expedition set out again in April of

1805, Charbonneau went with them, along with his young Native American wife, Sacagawea. She was a member of a tribe that lived far to the west, the Shoshone, although she had been kidnapped away from them at the age of 12 by an enemy tribe. Lewis and Clark knew that her knowledge of the Shoshone language and her memories of the land to the west would be very useful. They were pleased to welcome her to the expedition. She had just given birth to a baby boy, but she was not afraid. She would carry him on her back all the way to the Pacific Ocean.

Once again the Corps of Discovery paddled their boats upstream, floating into the country that would one day be the state of Montana. The Missouri River challenged them; they had to carry their boats around giant waterfalls and fight off the huge grizzly bears who hunted along its banks. A sudden spring storm on the river tipped one of their boats, and young Sacagawea earned the praise of all the men when she calmly swam into the river's waves and recovered all the gear that had spilled out. But still, despite these trials, boats seemed the best way to travel. In fact, Lewis and Clark confidently expected to be able to reach the Pacific Ocean by boat. They knew, of course, that there were mountains in the west; they expected that they would need to do a bit of climbing up and over the Continental Divide, but they assumed that they would then find large rivers flowing out toward the Pacific. They did not expect—they could not have expected—the immensity of the Rocky Mountains.

Late in the afternoon on May 26, Lewis climbed up a hillside shadowing the riverbank. When he reached the summit, he stopped short in wonder, for there, he said, "I beheld the Rocky Mountains for the first time . . . [They] were covered with snow and the sun shone on it in such a manner as to give me the most . . . plain and satisfactory view . . . but when I reflected on the difficulties which this snowy barrier would most probably throw in my way to the Pacific, and the sufferings and hardships of myself and party in them, it in some measure counterbalanced the joy I had felt in the first moments in which I gazed on them."

A snowy barrier, indeed. Lewis and Clark realized that this was no simple up-and-over. This was a trek requiring hundreds of miles and many, many weeks. Their boats were useless; they would need horses, instead, as well as some sort of guidance to prevent them from becoming hopelessly lost in the maze of valleys and peaks.

They found a nearby Native camp while seeking to buy horses, but they didn't have much hope. After all, they would need many horses, not just one or two, and why would the Natives be willing to part with so many? But then as they entered the camp, a cry of joy startled them. Sacagawea had caught sight of the Native's leader and burst into happy tears. It was her own brother! This was the very tribe from whom she had been stolen as a child. Now in this most fortunate of circumstances, she had been reunited with her family. She could introduce her little son to them and also encourage them to sell to the expedition all the horses they needed.

And so they climbed the cold and barren mountains, following the Natives' advice and crossing the Continental Divide where Lewis paused to drink from a stream that would reach the ocean. When their food ran low, Sacagawea helped them find edible roots and plants that gave them the strength to go on. They built canoes and descended the mountain streams until they reached the Columbia River, the greatest of western rivers. The expedition sighted the Pacific Ocean for the first time on November 7, 1805, setting foot on its wild beaches two weeks later. With another winter upon them, they faced the heavy task of building another camp, Fort Clatsop, where they huddled through months of wracking Pacific storms. Lewis spent the winter writing, filling his journals with memories of wondrous sights.

By March 22, 1806, the stormy weather had finally begun to gentle, and the following morning on March 23, the Corps began their journey homeward, using canoes to paddle upstream along the Columbia River and later trekking over land until they once again reached the familiar Missouri River where they bade farewell to Sacagawea and Charbonneau at Fort Mandan. Now, floating easily along with the current instead of laboriously paddling upstream, they traveled quickly, fetching up to the docks in St. Louis on September 23, 1806.

They had been gone for more than two years and traveled 8,000 miles. It was as if they had visited another world, filled with new and unknown plants and animals and a majestic landscape that defied description. They had not found the Northwest Passage: that dream was now and truly dead. But a new dream would arise in its place, a dream of the Wild West, where anything was possible, where the mountains scraped the sky and the rivers flowed with gold and a man could taste the ocean in a clear-flowing stream.

Chapter 27

Over the Pathless Oceans

The Navigations of Nathaniel Bowditch

Suppose with me that one of your friends has come to spend the day at your house. The summer sun is hot, and the two of you decide to make an excursion to a nearby park—perhaps it has a shaded basketball court or a pool full of cool water. "But," your friend might say, "I've never been to that park. I don't know how to get there."

"It's okay," you might reply. "I know the way."

And so you set out confidently; you know what streets to follow and which corners to turn. You point out the landmarks along the route to your friend: the ice-cream shop, the fire station, a huge gnarled oak. In just a short while, the two of you are playing ball or plunging off the pool's diving board, having safely found your way. The next time your friend visits the neighborhood, he will be able to follow your landmarks and find the park on his own.

But now suppose that you and your friend would like to enjoy a park that's new to both of you; neither of you have been there. Thankfully, though, your dad has a map of the neighborhood, which clearly shows the park's location. You might have to pause for a moment at some of the street corners to double check that you're turning the right way, but the map shows you where you need to go, and soon you're at the park. When you decide to head home, the journey back is easy; you and your friend both remember the landmarks and street names you passed on the way there.

In both of these situations, you have been a *navigator*: a person who finds his way from one place to another either through personal knowledge of the destination or through using a map that someone else has drawn.

But what if there were no map? What if you set out for the park with only a vague idea of where it might be? And what if there were no landmarks to help you remember the way?

This was the challenge for sailors for most of the world's history. After all, landmarks are only useful if you can see the land. At sea, once you sail beyond the horizon and leave the shore behind, all you can see for miles in any direction is the rippling surface of the ocean with the sun, or the stars at night, overhead. You can't be sure where you are; the water around you all looks the same. Nevertheless, over the centuries, mankind ventured out upon the oceans, finding his way with different methods of navigation.

One of these methods was called *dead reckoning*. To do this, a ship's captain would use a *compass*—a device that shows which direction you are going—to keep the ship moving forward in a straight line. Then he would measure the ship's speed using a long rope along which knots had been tied. A piece of wood was fastened at its end, and one of the sailors would heave this wooden weight into the sea. Another sailor, loosely gripping the rope, counted the knots as they passed through his hands, while yet another man timed the whole operation using a tiny, 30-second hourglass. The number of knots counted along the rope in that 30-second timespan measured the speed of the ship. Columbus's ship, the *Santa Maria*, sailed along at about 4 *knots* for most of his voyage, which is about four and a half miles every hour; a dolphin chasing a school of herring can swim as fast as

18 knots; a battleship during the years of World War II would travel at 30 knots or so.

Once the captain knew his speed, he made a note on a chart of the distance he had traveled in a certain direction. These charts were meticulously drawn by hundreds of ship captains over many, many voyages, showing the speed and distance to many destinations. This is how so many people were able to follow after Columbus and Cabot and the other explorers. This was also why Columbus was very brave: he set out into the west with only a bare suggestion—Toscanelli's map—of where he was going.

In addition to dead reckoning, though, sailors could also use the sky. Though the ocean is flat and featureless, the sky is an ever-changing panorama, and sailors had known since ancient times that the patterns of the sun, moon, and stars repeated themselves and could be used for navigation, particularly to find a ship's latitude. You might remember that the lines of latitude are the imaginary lines on the earth's surface that run parallel to the equator. To find latitude, sailors could use a device called an astrolabe, which measured the angle from an object in the sky—the sun or the North Star—down to the horizon. Using that measurement and a set of elaborate tables, a ship's navigator could know just how far to the north or south from the equator he had come. This method of finding your way is called *celestial navigation*.

But, as you might imagine, neither of these methods were foolproof or entirely accurate. Winds or heavy currents could pull a ship off course and, thus, ruin any attempt at dead reckoning. A stormy sky could hide the stars so that the captain was sailing blindly forward with no recourse to celestial navigation. By the year 1800, as more and more ships were crossing the oceans, the need for a more accurate way to navigate across them had become clear. But, how to do it? Solving such a large and complex problem would require a marvelous, ingenious mind.

Happily, in Salem, Massachusetts, such a mind existed inside the head of a young man named Nathaniel Bowditch.

He was born in 1773, the fourth of seven children. His father, Habakkuk Bowditch, was often away at sea, and the family was poor and burdened, for Nathaniel's mother, Mary, was very sick. She died when Nathaniel was but 10 years old; his brothers and sisters were sent away to various friends and relations, and young Nathaniel was apprenticed to a ship *chandler*—a person who provided the great, many-sailed ships with all the things that they might need for a voyage: cloth, tar, oil, rope, tools. For the next 11 years, Nathaniel would labor in the chandlery, but, though his body was cooped up there, his mind was not.

Nathaniel loved mathematics. Because he could not go to school, he gave himself the task of learning everything he could. At the age of 14, he taught himself algebra; two years later, he had mastered *calculus* as well—difficult, advanced mathematics that uses numbers and symbols to describe things that are constantly changing, like the orbits of planets out in space or the movement of water in a stream. He learned to read Latin, ancient as it was, because that was the language that filled the great scientific books of Sir Isaac Newton and Johannes Kepler, and Nathaniel wanted to read them. He was always reading, whenever he could, and he was fortunate, for books were available in Salem even from unexpected sources. One day, for example, a privateer—a pirate, really—sailed into Salem's harbor and delivered into the town a whole library of books that he had taken from a ship off the coast of England. Wonderful books they were, books in English, French, Latin, and Spanish. Nathaniel mastered them all, learning the languages and devouring the books. By the time he was 21, he was one of the most highly educated people in America—and all through his own efforts and in the time he could spare outside of his work.

In 1795, Nathaniel went to sea as a ship's clerk and record-keeper. Now, at that time, most seafarers were using a book called *The Practical Navigator* to find their way on the ocean. It was filled with printed tables that showed the locations of stars and the movements of tides. But, as their voyage progressed, Nathaniel began to feel uneasy about the information in the book. He started to make his own calculations using his long-stored-up wealth of knowledge and study, and he realized quickly that *The Practical Navigator* was not so practical after all. It was filled with errors, thousands of them. Day by day, as the waves whispered along the ship's hull, as the ship completed its voyage and Nathaniel set out on another and then another excursion, he re-computed the tables in the book, penciled in corrections, and added new calculations and more accurate charts. He even figured out a way to take more accurate measurements for celestial navigation by observing the moon and comparing it to the position of a fixed star or of the sun. By the time he was done in 1802, he had completely re-written the book, so much so that it was published as an entirely new work, *The New American Practical Navigator.*

Nathaniel's book was extraordinary, not only because it was so much more accurate, but also because it was easy to read and understand. Nathaniel had determined in his heart that he would not put anything in his book that he could not teach every member of a ship's crew. By the end of his final voyage, he had taught everyone on the ship, including the cook, to take a measurement of the moon and stars and then determine the ship's position on a chart.

In the years that followed, Nathaniel wrote many more astounding things about astronomy, mathematics, and navigation: papers about stars and comets and swinging pendulums and the fiery tracks of falling meteors. He continued to read and learn all his life; his home library in Salem housed more than 2,500 books, 29 of them written by his own hand. But of course the most famous of all his works is *The New American Practical Navigator,* a book so well written and so accurate that it is still found aboard American ships, even to this day, where most sailors simply refer to it by its author's name: "Bowditch." The United States government continues to update and publish it even today, making it available to all. This would surely have pleased Nathaniel, who wanted so dearly to make navigation something that any person can learn.

The New American Practical Navigator *by Nathaniel Bowditch*

Nathaniel died in 1838. The monument erected above his grave shows him seated, looking into the far distance, with a book in his hands. The sailors of Salem offered him this tribute:

> *As long as ships shall sail, the needle points to the north, and the stars go through their wonted courses in the heavens, the name of Dr. Bowditch will be revered as of one who has helped his fellow men in a time of need, who was and is a guide to them over the pathless ocean, and of one who forwarded the great interests of mankind.*

Statue of Nathaniel Bowditch in Salem, Massachusetts

Chapter 28

"Don't Give Up The Ship"

The War of 1812

Captain Oliver Hazard Perry stood at the prow of his ship, the *Lawrence*, and knew that he had come to the end. Around him, the clear blue water of Lake Erie was pockmarked with smoking debris smashed from the deck and hull of his ship by a hail of cannon fire. The *Lawrence* was a battered wreck, her hull breached with a dozen jagged rents, her big iron guns destroyed. Her deck was littered with fallen men, many groaning from the pain of their wounds and many dead. Ahead, through drifts of smoke, he could see the enemy: hulking English warships, the mouths of their cannons threatening his helpless ship with total destruction.

This was the end: the *Lawrence* could fight no longer.

But the captain lifted his eyes from the scene of death and ruin before him. There, far above the deck, he could see a flash of deep blue: his personal battle flag, stitched for him just the day before by the women of a nearby town. A plain blue rectangle, it bore five bold words: "Don't Give Up the Ship."

Perry squared his shoulders. His ship might be defeated, but he was not! The battle had not yet been lost. Turning sharply, he gestured to his few remaining men and strode forward, a new plan taking shape in his mind, a fiery determination in the gleam of his eyes. The day might be grim, the odds might be long, but he could not, nor would he ever, give up.

Though Captain Perry did not know it, the action that he was about to take would be the turning point in a war that had been going very badly—America's second war for independence, her second struggle to counter the military might of England—the War of 1812. How this war came about, and how Perry came to be battling English warships on the waters of an American lake, is a story filled with anger and humiliation and, ultimately, hope.

The story begins, not with the stalwart determination of one young American captain, but instead with the burning ambition of Napoleon Bonaparte, emperor of France.

You see, after selling Louisiana to the United States in 1803, Napoleon had turned all his thoughts toward one goal: expanding France's empire until it encompassed all of Europe. By 1805, with victories over the Russians and the Austrians, he was making great strides toward achieving that dream, and yet, always, one nation stood in his way: England, his fiercest enemy. And, though Napoleon's armies had ruled much of the land, England—with her mighty navy, her skilled captains, and cannon-bedecked warships—England had been master of the seas. France and England fought on land and ocean, over and over, but neither could gain the mastery.

The United States wanted nothing to do with any of this; she wanted to remain *neutral*. With French and English ships called away to war, American merchants and seafarers were making enormous profits, quietly going about their business, running the trade routes between North America and the Caribbean and the nations of Europe. But England soon put a stop to that in ways that were cruelly unjust.

English ships began interfering with American trade. They would seize American ships that were docked in England and confiscate all of the trade goods aboard. They would stop American ships at sea and kidnap the sailors on board and force them to work on English ships, a practice called *impressment*. And then, in the summer of 1807, an English ship, the *Leopold*, ran across an American vessel, the *Chesapeake*. When the *Chesapeake*'s captain refused to allow his ship to be boarded and his sailors taken, the *Leopold* fired its cannons. Three Americans were killed, and the ship was forced to surrender her men.

As you can imagine, the American people were outraged. How dare they! The United States and England were not at war; why was England acting as if they were? A growing murmur spread: perhaps we should be!

President Jefferson counseled patience. He attempted to reason with the English government, and, when that was unsuccessful, he tried to short-circuit England's aggressive actions by stopping all foreign trade in the United States. No goods coming in, no goods going out. England couldn't attack American ships if they weren't out on the oceans.

But, of course, that didn't work either, because American merchants loudly objected. Foreign trade was far too profitable; they couldn't just give it up! So, the next president, James Madison, tried a different approach: he renewed trade with most of the world, but forbade it with France and England as long as they were at war.

Still the kidnapping of sailors and the seizing of ships continued.

Meanwhile, out on the American frontier, a different sort of trouble was brewing. In the years following the War for Independence, the land west of the Appalachian Mountains had been set aside by President John Adams for Native tribes, for their homes and hunting grounds. But more and more Americans were crossing the mountains, wanting land to build their own homes and farms. The Natives were asked, over and over, to sign new agreements and give up more of their land. Some of the tribes were growing angry and restless, watching the land they'd been promised disappear. By 1811, that anger had become a spear in the hands of one man, a powerful Native American leader named Tecumseh.

Tecumseh realized that the Natives would face only defeat and chaos unless they could all come together, not as many different tribes but as one Native nation. He convinced the leaders of other tribes to join with him in insisting that no new land agreements could be signed unless all the tribes agreed to it.

Tecumseh's native union, and his fiery, angry speeches rallying the Natives together, worried the governor of the frontier territory, General William Henry Harrison. He gathered a thousand of his soldiers into a camp near Tecumseh's capital on the Tippecanoe River. Although Tecumseh had warned them to stay peaceful, the Natives there attacked Harrison's men, killing many of them. When Harrison returned the attack, the Native town was burned and all of their supplies and stockpiled food destroyed. Destroyed, too, was Tecumseh's plans for a united Native nation; he fled to Canada, seeking protection from the English forces there and allying himself with England.

In all of this unrest, though, the Americans saw more than just Tecumseh's persuasive voice. It had long been suspected that English spies were circulating among the Natives, encouraging them to attack American settlers. When this suspicion was piled on top of the news of kidnapped sailors and stolen trade goods, the calls for justice and vengeance grew ever louder.

So it was that, on June 18, 1812, the United States declared war upon England.

War with England once again! The Americans were ill-prepared for it. Since the days of the Revolutionary War, the army had shrunk to just a few thousand men who were badly trained and sparsely equipped. The American navy was in better shape with well-built ships, but there were only 16 of them. There was little money—the years of English interference in American trade had seen to that. Facing the English military might, the Americans had their righteous anger, but little more.

In the first year of the war, the little American army won no battles and gained no ground. They tried three times to advance into Canada and beat the English there, but each attempt failed dismally; and then to make matters worse, by 1813 English warships had *blockaded* the American coast, trapping most of the American navy, such as it was, in port.

With the oceans closed and Canada still firmly English, there seemed to be only one other opportunity: control of America's inland seas, the Great Lakes. The English navy controlled four of the lakes, patrolling Lake Erie with a squadron of proud warships. They were not expecting any sort of challenge.

But then, they were not expecting Oliver Hazard Perry.

Captain Perry had requested command of America's naval forces on Lake Erie and, upon arriving there in the summer of 1813, had spent weeks felling trees and building ships out of the fresh lumber. By September he felt ready to try the mettle of his little fleet. Aboard his flagship, the *Lawrence*, he sailed out in search of the English ships, and he found them on September 10 at a place along Lake Erie's shore called Put-in-Bay. He ordered his men to prepare for battle, and, as they did, he turned to one of his officers and said, "This is the most important day of my life."

For four hours the English warships pummeled the *Lawrence*, their powerful cannons ripping her apart, until only eight men and Perry himself were left standing. But the motto stitched onto his battle flag burned fiercely in Perry's heart: "Don't Give Up the Ship." And so instead of surrendering, which is certainly what the English captains expected him to do, he leaped into a nearby rowboat, his few faithful men at his heels, and rowed across a half-mile of open lake, cannonballs and bullets whistling over his head, to take command of another ship in his fleet, the *Niagara*.

Though he was wounded and bleeding, he ordered the *Niagara's* helmsman to turn her about and steer her directly between the oncoming warships. With her cannons blazing, the

Niagara broke through the English line, dealing such a shattering blow that, within just a few minutes, every English ship lowered its flag in defeat. It was the first time in history that an entire English naval squadron had surrendered.

Back aboard the ruin of the *Lawrence*, Perry accepted the English officers' surrender, and then hastily composed a note to General Harrison, who was gathering his forces on the shores of Lake Champlain. "We have met the enemy," Perry wrote, "and they are ours."

As soon as General Harrison received this message, he knew that the English would be moving. With Lake Erie now in American hands, the English troops clustered here and there around the Great Lakes would be cut off from support. They would try to retreat north to more friendly ground in Canada. General Harrison set his men to marching, hoping to intercept them. On the morning of October 5th, he met the retreating army on the banks of the Thames River in the land that is now Ontario, in Canada. Alongside the English troops was the Native American leader Tecumseh with a band of his warriors.

The battle was short and fierce. The American soldiers drove the English into retreat and then faced Tecumseh and his warriors. In the fighting that followed, the Native leader was killed, and his warriors lost heart. When Tecumseh died, so too died the dream of a Native Union.

For the Americans, though, the victories won by Captain Perry and General Harrison brought hope and turned the course of the war. With control of the Great Lakes, America regained control of the Ohio Valley and all her frontier lands. The English had been forced into a humiliating retreat. There would still be dark times, as we will see in the next chapter, but a torch had been lit. The path forward could be seen. They could see what must be done: keep pressing forward, keep looking for ways to win.

Don't Give Up the Ship.

Chapter 29

By the Dawn's Early Light

America's Day

Napoleon Bonaparte's plan had always been to fold all of Europe into one great French Empire. But in 1814 those hopes were forever dashed. He was defeated in battle, removed from his throne, and exiled from France to the little island of Elba in the Mediterranean Sea. This was joyous tidings for most of Europe, and especially for England, but it was terrible news for the United States. With Napoleon gone and the war with France finished, England was free to focus her attention solely upon the upstart Americans.

So it was that, in the summer of 1814, an English fleet sailed into Chesapeake Bay with 5,000 soldiers aboard. On the evening of August 24, the redcoats swarmed ashore, swatted aside an attack by American soldiers at the town of Bladensburg, about five miles from Washington, D.C., and then marched into the capital. Their orders were clear: "destroy and lay waste" and teach these Americans a stern lesson. With that goal in mind, the English troops made for the United States Capitol Building, the home of America's Congress.

Surrounding the building, the redcoats set fire to its southern wing. The flames spread with frightening speed, licking greedily through the halls and then roaring in triumph as all the books and papers in the Library of Congress caught fire. The wooden floors and ceilings burned, and the glass skylights and windows melted in the intense heat. In just a few hours, the beautiful Capitol building was lost.

Now the English troops marched up Pennsylvania Avenue toward the White House (then called the Presidential Mansion). President James Madison wasn't there—he had hurried toward Bladensburg upon receiving news of the battle there—but his wife, Dolley, was preparing to share some dinner with friends. The urgent warning came at the last minute, as the English were even then bearing down on the Mansion, and *The First Lady* was compelled to flee, pausing only to stuff some of the valuable silverware into a carrying bag, while the doorkeeper lifted a precious portrait of George Washington down from one wall and hurried it to safety.

Dolley had scarcely fled through one door when the English entered through another. They laughed in haughty amusement at finding the table laid and the wine glasses already filled, and they sat themselves down and ate all of Dolley's dinner. Then they took their torches from room to room and set the president's home ablaze.

Throughout that dark night, Washington burned. The English piled the fuel high, wanting the fires to smolder and spread. But in that intent, at least, they were defeated, for the next day violent thunderstorms drenched the city and doused the fires. The cold rain dampened the redcoats' enthusiasm for further destruction, and they returned to their ships. The entire fleet set out once more, sailing north toward Baltimore with the intent of assaulting that city and burning it too. The English hated Baltimore, because it was the home port for many of America's *privateers;* their bold attacks on English ships had earned them a fearsome reputation. The destruction of Baltimore would deal a severe blow to the Americans and give the English great satisfaction.

The defense of Baltimore was undertaken by Major General Samuel Smith, a fierce old man who had been a hero of the Revolutionary War and commander of the state's militia. He had never backed down from a battle in his life, and he was determined to foil the English in every possible way. He stationed 13,000 men, soldiers and citizens alike, along the heights around the city. He put the rest of Baltimore's people to work, digging trenches for shelter, maneuvering cannons into place, loading muskets, and piling up ammunition. He barred the mouth of Baltimore Harbor with a long, jagged line of sunken ships to deny entrance to any English warships.

Baltimore Harbor was guarded as well by a star-shaped fortress called Fort McHenry. It was manned by a thousand soldiers commanded by Major George Armistead. He had, early in the war, ordered an enormous American flag to be raised above the fort, a flag with 15 red and white stripes and 15 white stars—15 because, in those days, the United States was adding a new stripe and a new star for each new state, and Vermont and Kentucky had just been added to the Union. This huge banner was 30 feet wide and 42 feet long; "so large," Armistead declared, "the British will have no difficulty seeing it from a distance."

The English commanders planned to attack Baltimore from two directions: the army would attack by land; the English fleet would sail right up to the city's docks, raining cannon fire all the while. But the English army met with much stiffer opposition than they had been expecting. The city's borders were guarded by a hundred cannons and thousands of armed defenders, forcing the redcoats to retreat. Another attack would be too dangerous, the English decided. They would wait for the help of the warships and their deadly cannons.

But when the English ships entered the harbor, they were confronted with three unusual sights: Armistead's giant flag, waving defiantly above the walls of Fort McHenry; the barrier of sunken wrecks, preventing them from sailing closer to the city;

and, strangely, a little ship, skimming toward them as fast as it could sail, flying a white flag of *truce*.

Aboard the ship was a young lawyer named Francis Scott Key.

Francis Scott Key had been busy. He had fought alongside the American soldiers at Bladensburg, watched in horror as Washington went up in flames, and then received the terrible news that a friend of his, Dr. William Beanes, had been captured by the English and was being held aboard the flagship of the English fleet, the *Tonnant*. Key gathered some documents to use in Dr. Beanes's defense and then hurried to Baltimore, riding through the night. Down at the docks, he boarded a little ship, the *Minden*, and, with its white flag flying, sailed out to intercept the oncoming English fleet.

The *Tonnant*'s captain, Sir Alexander Cochrane, allowed the *Minden* to draw near and, after hearing the reason for Key's bold approach, agreed to hear his plea on behalf of his friend. Taking a deep breath, Key marshaled his arguments: Dr. Beanes was a man of peace whose only cause was to help the sick and wounded. He could not possibly be considered a threat to the English; in fact, he had often tended to English soldiers. Then, as the captain was shaking his head doubtfully, Key pulled out the documents he had brought: letters from English prisoners of war that described Dr. Beanes's kindness to them and of his skill as a doctor.

The letters persuaded the captain; he agreed to free Dr. Beanes and allow him to return with Key to the *Minden*. But, he said, his voice growling a warning: There you must stay. You have observed all of our preparations for the battle to come; you have counted our ships and our weapons, and if you return to Baltimore, you would no doubt tell the defenders there everything you have seen here today. So you will share dinner with me tonight, and then you will return to the *Minden*, which will remain anchored right where she is until this battle is done.

For 25 hours, all through that day and long into the night, the English warships bombarded Fort McHenry with cannon shells and gunpowder rockets, doing their best to pound the fort into surrender. The English army lurked—menacingly—on the outskirts of the city, ready to surge forward and attack as soon as the fort fell. On board the *Minden*, Dr. Beanes and Francis Scott Key watched, peering anxiously through the thick darkness, on the lookout for a glimmer of stars and stripes in the flares of light from exploding bombs and cannon fire. They knew that if the flag came down, it would mean that the fort had been taken and the battle lost.

But when at last the early light of dawn silvered the sky, the flag was still there! Stained with battle smoke, tattered by gunfire, but still waving proudly, the flag shouted out across the harbor that the fort had not fallen, the city had not been taken, the battle had not been lost. It was America's day.

The sight of that flag took the heart out of the English. Baltimore would not fall into their hands. That morning, the soldiers on the city's borders withdrew, and the English fleet turned sail and retreated. They turned their attention to the south, to the city of New Orleans, but there, too, they met only defeat and disaster. After the Battle of Baltimore, the English came to realize that this war with the United States was not worth the cost—in men, in money, and in pride. On Christmas Eve of 1814, England and the United States signed a peace treaty ending the War of 1812.

The war ended, but the memory of that long, anxious night has endured. Francis Scott Key, his thoughts overflowing with the memory of what he had seen, spent the next day composing a poem. He captured in words the joy and heart-swelling pride that he had felt.

This is what he wrote:

The Star-Spangled Banner

O say can you see, by the dawn's early light,
What so proudly we hail'd at the twilight's last gleaming,
Whose broad stripes and bright stars through the perilous fight
O'er the ramparts we watch'd were so gallantly streaming?
And the rocket's red glare, the bombs bursting in air,
Gave proof through the night that our flag was still there,
O say does that star-spangled banner yet wave
O'er the land of the free and the home of the brave?

On the shore dimly seen through the mists of the deep
Where the foe's haughty host in dread silence reposes,
What is that which the breeze, o'er the towering steep,
As it fitfully blows, half conceals, half discloses?
Now it catches the gleam of the morning's first beam,
In full glory reflected now shines in the stream,
'Tis the star-spangled banner - O long may it wave
O'er the land of the free and the home of the brave!

And where is that band who so vauntingly swore,
That the havoc of war and the battle's confusion
A home and a Country should leave us no more?
Their blood has wash'd out their foul footstep's pollution.
No refuge could save the hireling and slave
From the terror of flight or the gloom of the grave,
And the star-spangled banner in triumph doth wave
O'er the land of the free and the home of the brave.

O thus be it ever when freemen shall stand
Between their lov'd home and the war's desolation!
Blest with vict'ry and peace may the heav'n rescued land
Praise the power that hath made and preserv'd us a nation!
Then conquer we must, when our cause it is just,
And this be our motto—"In God is our trust,"
And the star-spangled banner in triumph shall wave
O'er the land of the free and the home of the brave.

All Americans can share the pride so lovingly expressed in that poem. The land of the free and the home of the brave—this is the United States of America through the years of its history, in the days when only the Natives were here and through the intrepid voyages of the explorers, in the quiet courage of the first colonists, braving the unknown continent to build homes for themselves. Those colonies joined together, yearning for liberty from a faraway king. They fought bravely to earn that freedom and then to accept the enormous challenge of inventing their own government and safeguarding it with a Constitution the likes of which the world had never seen. Then, in the War of 1812, the young nation showed itself resolute and strong. The American day had well and truly dawned, and its sun would continue to rise.

More than 200 years later, here we are in the land of the free and the home of the brave, still rejoicing to be a part of that same America, working to preserve our precious Union.

Together, we the people are sharing that same American day.

Routes of the principal explorers of the United States

Glossary

adobe. A building material made by mixing wet clay with straw. It is often formed into bricks that are baked hard in the sun.

alliance. A formal agreement establishing friendship and cooperation.

amendment. A change, such as an addition to or a deletion from a law or to a constitution. In the United States, the Constitution can be amended only if three-fourths of the state legislatures agree.

Anglican. Someone or something that is part of the Church of England.

Arctic Circle. A line of *latitude* that circles the northernmost part of the earth. The Arctic Circle does not have a fixed position but instead marks those regions encircling the North Pole where, for at least 24 hours of every year, the sun does not set below the horizon. All of the land and water north of this line is called the Arctic.

assembly. In colonial America, a group of men elected by the people of a colony. The assembly was responsible for representing the interests of the colony and pleading its cause to the royal authorities. They met together to discuss the issues that concerned the colony and form solutions to the colony's problems. They took care of the colony's taxes and passed its laws.

blockade. A line of enemy ships or troops that prevents any entrance or exit.

charter. A formal document bestowed upon a person or group by a king or other governing official. In colonial America, a charter gave the person who held it permission to govern a certain territory and establish settlements there. A charter gave a colony the legal right to exist.

chunkey. A game played by Native Americans. It involved throwing or sliding a decorated stick toward a rolling hoop or disc, attempting to land the stick as close as possible to the disc as it stopped rolling and fell over.

clan. A group within a larger *tribe*, formed of people who belong to the same extended family and share a common ancestor.

colony. A group of people who build a settlement in another land or territory and claim that land for their original country. The original country rules the new settlement, which itself is also called a colony.

commandeer. To seize something without payment for public or military use.

confederation. A collection of independent groups who have united together in pursuit of some common purpose.

congress. A group of people meeting together in order to make laws. In the United States, Congress has two houses; that is, two separate groups are *elected* by the people to represent them. These houses are the House of Representatives, with a different number of Congressmen from each state based upon that state's population, and the Senate, with two Congressmen from every state, regardless of its population. In order for an idea to become a law, it must be approved by both houses of Congress and signed by the president.

continental divide. A mountain ridge that separates the flow of water in a continent. In North America, the continental divide runs north and south and is found in the Rocky Mountains: streams that flow down the east side of the divide end up in the Arctic Ocean, the Gulf of Mexico and the Atlantic Ocean, while streams flowing down the west side eventually reach the Pacific Ocean. Continental divides are found on every continent on earth.

contiguous United States. The whole of the country spread across North America from the Atlantic to the Pacific but not including the states of Hawaii and Alaska, since they are set apart from the rest of the states by a broad expanse of land and sea.

delegate. A person chosen by a larger group to represent them and speak or vote for them at a meeting or conference.

delta. A wetland area that forms as the mouth of a river spreads out and empties into a larger body of water such as an ocean. It is usually shaped like a giant triangle and so takes its name from the fourth letter of the Greek alphabet, the delta, which is written as a triangle. A delta is very flat, and the river divides into smaller branches as it flows over it.

diplomat. Someone who has been chosen by his or her government to represent his or her nation to other nations. A diplomat must use skill and tact to make the desires and needs of his country clear to foreign leaders and to forge agreements and alliances with them.

dissent. To disagree; to express an opinion contrary to that of those who are in authority or who are in the majority.

duty. A kind of tax that must be paid by the importer, or purchaser, whenever trade goods are brought into a country from another country. Governments use duty taxes to raise money, to protect their own farmers and merchants from being driven out of business by cheaper goods coming into the country from elsewhere, and to control the flow of goods in and out of the country.

estuary. A place along a coastline where freshwater from a river mixes with saltwater from the ocean. It is usually surrounded by wetlands and marshes.

election. The process of choosing someone, by voting, to be a political leader or a *representative* in the government.

federal government. A nation's central or general government, which takes care of things that impact the nation as a whole, such as funding the army or building the interstate roadways.

First Lady. The honorary title traditionally given to the wife of the president of the United States.

freedom of religion. The freedom to practice any religion or none at all, as one's beliefs dictate. Freedom of religion also means that the government does not intrude upon the practice of religion and does not establish an official church that citizens are required to attend.

frontier. The wild lands beyond the furthest edge of a country's settled and civilized regions.

geography. The study of the Earth's surface: its countries and people, its deserts, forests, mountains, seas and rivers, its climate and atmosphere, its seven continents and five oceans.

geyser. A spring or pool of water that has been heated by magma under the earth's crust. It sometimes erupts, throwing steam and boiling water high into the air. Some geysers deposit minerals around themselves and form a cone like a miniature volcano. The term *geyser* comes from the Icelandic word *geysir,* which means "to gush." Geysers are often found in company with *hot springs,* which are pools that do not erupt, and *fumaroles,* which emit only gasses and steam. Yellowstone National Park has the largest concentration of these geologic wonders in the entire world.

heretic. Someone who is part of a church or a religion but whose actions or opinions oppose its established teachings.

isthmus. A narrow strip of land that connects two larger landmasses.

kiva. An underground or partly underground room in a Pueblo village used for religious ceremonies or council meetings. A kiva was usually circular, and many included a *sipapu,* which is a hole dug near the north wall; it signifies the place where, in the ancient Puebloans' belief, the first people emerged from the underworld.

lacrosse. A game played by Native Americans that involved tossing a small ball from player to player using long, netted sticks.

latitude and longitude. Imaginary lines drawn on maps and globes for the purpose of easily locating places on Earth. The Earth is a sphere that rotates around an *axis* in the same way a spinning top spins. The North Pole is at one end of the axis, the South Pole is at the other end, and the equator runs around the middle like a belt. The lines of latitude run parallel to the equator; therefore, latitude shows how far north or south of the equator a location might be. The lines of longitude run around the globe in vertical rings meeting at the poles. Longitude thus indicates how far east or west one has traveled. Any spot on earth can be described by its degree of latitude and longitude. These measurements are called *coordinates.*

legislature. A group of people who are *elected* to their positions and have the authority to make laws. The word comes from two Latin words: *legis* and *lator,* which together mean "proposer of a law."

Silk Road. An interconnected network of trade routes that linked Europe and Asia. The Silk Road took its name from the silk fabric brought out of Asia and much desired in Europe. Merchants made use of the Silk Road beginning in ancient times and throughout the Middle Ages.

sphere. A three-dimensional object with no edges, which means that it is shaped like a ball. Every point on the surface of a sphere is equally distant from the sphere's center.

strait. A narrow channel of water that connects two larger bodies of water.

trade. The buying and selling of goods (things that people grow or create) and services (things that people do that are beneficial to others). *Domestic trade* happens within a single nation or group of people, and *international trade* occurs between and among different nations.

trading company. A group of people who pool their money to engage in trade, exploration, and colonization. Each member of a trading company shares in the risk: if their ventures do not succeed, they will lose all of the money that they originally *invested*; but if their ventures are successful, they will split all of the profits. Investments in a trading company are called *shares* or *stocks*. A company like this is called a *corporation*, because it is made up of a group of people who share the same goals and purpose, and the group acts as one *corporate*—that is, one united or combined—body.

tribe. A group composed of many families, or clans, who share the same ancestry, culture, and language.

truce. An agreement on both sides of a battle to stop fighting. Truces are usually temporary, but they can lead to an *armistice*, an agreement to permanently stop the war. A flag of truce is white, flown to indicate that the person holding it and approaching the opposing group has no hostile intention.

Endnotes

Ch. 1: An American Day

1. The distance from the sun to the earth, which averages nearly 93 million miles, is called an *astronomical unit.*

Ch. 3: Toscanelli's Map

1. Toscanelli's letter for King Alfonso V is dated June 25, 1474. It is written in Latin, and a number of different English translations can be found. The quotation from that letter in this chapter is taken from *Christopher Columbus: His Life, His Travels* by Jose Maria Asensio, a 19th-century Spanish historian.

   An English translation of the quotation is here:

   Henry Vignaud, *Toscanelli and Columbus: The Letter and Chart of Toscanelli on the Route to the Indies by Way of the West* (London: Sands & Co., 1902), 306, archive.org/details/toscanelliandco00vigngoog/page/n326/mode/2up.

Ch. 4: Searching for Cipango

1. The quotation from Toscanelli's letter to Columbus is taken from an English translation of the original letter, which Columbus had carefully copied into his journal.

   Columbus, *Journal,* 10.

2. Columbus described the people he met in great detail; a very small portion of that description was quoted in this chapter.

   Columbus, *Journal,* 38 and 39.

3. Columbus's thoughts about the island upon which they had landed are noted in his journal, as well as his urgent desire to leave at once and continue to seek for Japan.

   Columbus, *Journal,* 40.

Ch. 5: The Fourth Part of the World

1. The original letters patent bestowed upon Cabot by Henry VII is kept safe in the Public Records Office in London. The text can be viewed online at the following link:

   "Patent Granted by King Henry VII to John Cabot and his Sons, March 1496," Heritage: Newfoundland & Labrador, 2022, www.heritage.nf.ca/articles/exploration/1496-cabot-patent.php.

2. Sebastian Cabot drew a large and detailed map of the world, and his description of the Natives and wildlife of Newfoundland can be found in his written legend there. The map currently resides in the Norman B. Leventhal Map and Education Center at the Boston Public Library:

   Sebastian Cabot, cartographer, *World map of A.D. 1544 (the Sebastian-Cabot map)*, 1544, 53 x 90 cm, Norman B. Leventhal Map & Education Center at the Boston Public Library, collections.leventhalmap.org/search/commonwealth:7h149v62n

   An English translation of Cabot's legends, along with a copy of the map, is here:

   Douglas Brymner, *Report on Canadian Archives* (Ottawa, 1898), 119 and 127, archive.org/details/reportoncanadian1897publ/page/n147/mode/2up.

3. John Cabot's assertion that London would become a "depot of spices" is found in a letter written by a fellow Italian, reporting somewhat spitefully on Cabot's remarks to a Duke back in Italy.

   Columbus, *Journal,* 205.

4. Amerigo Vespucci made his observations regarding the new continent in a letter to his patron, Lorenzo de Medici. His letters were published throughout Europe, causing a sensation and producing the unexpected result of Vespucci's giving his name to the entire continent.

   Vespucci, *Letters,* 42 and 44.

Ch. 7: The Last Voyage of the *Discovery*

1. Because Hudson's journals and records were delivered to the Dutch, only small portions of them have ever been published in English. Much of what we know about the voyages of the *Half Moon* come from the journals of one of her crewmen, Robert Juet, who was also one of the leaders of the mutiny on the *Discovery*. An excellent transcription of Juet's journal can be found here:

   Robert Juet, "Juet's Journal of Hudson's 1609 Voyage, from the 1625 edition of *Purchas His Pilgrimes,*" New Netherland Museum/Half Moon, last modified 2006, halfmoon.mus.ny.us/Juets-journal.pdf.

Ch. 8: The Lost Colony

1. White's mournful words about giving his family up to God were written in a letter to Richard Hakluyt, an English writer who promoted the colonization of the New World. I found them quoted in an interesting lecture given at the Jamestown Settlement Museum on July 19, 2008, by Professor Karen O. Kupperman. The text of that lecture can be found here:

   Karen O. Kupperman, "Roanoke's Achievements," Jamestown Settlement & American Revolution Museum at Yorktown, n.d., web.archive.org/web/20220817035855/https://jyfmuseums.org/exhibitions/collections-and-exhibitions/special-exhibitions/a-new-world/roanokes-achievement/.

Ch. 9: Work to Eat

1. John Smith's rule: "If a man will not work, he shall not eat."

   Edward Arber, ed., *Travels and Works of Captain John Smith* (Edinburgh: John Grant, 1910), 149, archive.org/details/b31359516_0001/page/148/mode/2up.

Ch. 10: Across the Vast and Furious Ocean

1. The full text of the Mayflower Compact may be found in many places online. I read it here:

   "Mayflower Compact: 1620," Yale Law School Lillian Goldman Law Library: The Avalon Project, last modified 2008, avalon.law.yale.edu/17th_century/mayflower.asp.

2. The quotation from William Bradford is taken from his history of the colony: Bradford, *Plymouth*, 55.

Ch. 11: New Amsterdam, New France, and New England

1. An interesting discussion regarding the meaning of "Manhattan" can be found here:

   Ives Goddard, "The Origin and Meaning of the Name 'Manhattan'," *New York History* 92, no. 4 (Oct. 2010): 277–293, repository.si.edu/bitstream/handle/10088/16790/anth_Manhattan.pdf.

2. The letter reporting the condition of the New Netherlands colonists was written by a man named Peter Schagen, dated November 7, 1626. A transcription of it can be found at the New Netherland Institute's website:

   "Peter Schagen Letter," New Netherland Institute, n.d., www.newnetherlandinstitute.org/history-and-heritage/additional-resources/dutch-treats/peter-schagen-letter/.

3. The quotation regarding the founding of Quebec was written by Samuel de Champlain in 1608. His entire account can be read at the Early Americas Digital Archives, maintained by the University of Maryland:

   "Founding of Quebec," Early Americas Digital Archive, n.d., eada.lib.umd.edu/text-entries/founding-of-quebec/.

4. John Winthrop's desire that the Puritans be a "city on a hill" comes from a verse in the Bible: Matthew 5:14 (ESV):

"You are the light of the world. A city set on a hill cannot be hidden."

Ch. 12: The Gifts of Charles II

1. An annotated transcript of the Rhode Island Royal Charter of 1663 can be found here:

   "Rhode Island's Royal Charter," Rhode Island Department of State, 2022, www.sos.ri.gov/divisions/civics-and-education/ for-educators/themed-collections/rhode-island-charter.

Ch. 13: Noble Experiments

1. Penn's comments regarding Pennsylvania's future as "the seed of a nation" are expressed in a letter that he wrote to a friend in 1681. I found it quoted here:

   Donehoo, *Pennsylvania,* 160.

2. The phrase "holy experiment" comes from William Penn's poetic musings about the nature of his colony:

   > *For my country, I eyed the Lord, in obtaining it;*
   > *And more was I drawn inward to look to him,*
   > *And to owe it to his hand and power, than to any other way;*
   > *I have so obtained it, and desire to keep it;*
   > *That I may not be unworthy of his love;*
   > *But do that, which may answer his kind Providence,*
   > *And serve his truth and people:*
   > *That an example may be set up to the nations:*
   > *There may be room there, though not here,*
   > *For such an holy experiment.*

   Edwin B. Bronner, *William Penn's "Holy Experiment": The Founding of Pennsylvania 1681–1701* (New York: Temple University Publications, 1962), 6, archive.org/details/ williampennsholy0000bron/page/6/mode/2up.

Ch. 14: The Charter Oak

1. The king's orders to Sir Edmund Andros are quoted here:

Gocher, *Wadsworth*, 277.

2. Robert Treat's impassioned words regarding the charter can be found in the same account:

Gocher, *Wadsworth*, 320 and 321.

3. The colonists' insistence that "They must & would have the Government in their own hands" is quoted by Stephen Saunders Webb in his book *Lord Churchill's Coup*, which discusses the worldwide impact of the Glorious Revolution in England:

Stephen Saunders Webb, *Lord Churchill's Coup: The Anglo-American Empire and the Glorious Revolution Reconsidered* (Syracuse, N.Y.: Syracuse University Press, 1998), 192, archive. org/details/lordchurchillsco0000webb/page/192/mode/2up.

Ch. 15: Black Sam Bellamy

1. In 1724, a man calling himself Captain Charles Johnson published a book called *A General History of the Robberies and Murders of the Most Notorious Pyrates*. He quotes in full a famous speech by Black Sam Bellamy in which he denounces the wealthy merchants as "scoundrels" and "villains." I've included a small portion of that speech in this chapter.

Daniel Defoe, *A General History of the Pyrates* (Mineola, NY: Dover Publications, 1999), 587, archive.org/details/ generalhistoryof0000defo_e1h9/page/586/mode/2up.

Ch. 16: "We Shall Know Better"

1. Thomas Jefferson's comments on the beauty of the Ohio River can be found in his *Notes on the State of Virginia*. I used the edition published by Penguin Classics, where this quotation is found on page 12.

Jefferson, *Notes*, 12.

2. George Washington's comment about the panicked behavior of the English soldiers was expressed in a letter to his mother

written on July 18, 1755. You can read the letter in full, along with many other wonderful things, at the National Archives "Founders Online":

"From George Washington to Mary Ball Washington, 18 July 1755," *Founders Online,* National Archives, founders.archives. gov/documents/Washington/02-01-02-0167. [Original source: W. W. Abbot, ed., *The Papers of George Washington*, Colonial Series, vol. 1, *7 July 1748–14 August 1755*, (Charlottesville: University Press of Virginia, 1983), 336–338.]

3. General Braddock's last words are recorded in a number of sources. One such:

Thomas E. Crocker, *Braddock's March* (Yardley, PA: Westholme Publishing, 2011), 234, archive.org/details/ braddocksmarchho0000croc/page/234/mode/2up.

Ch. 17: Farewell, Acadia

1. Pontiac's warning was directed at an agent tasked by General Gage with supervising England's relationship with the Natives. I found it quoted here:

Taylor, *American Colonies,* 437.

Ch. 18: Poor Richard

1. Franklin's words regarding freedom of speech can be found in the eighth Silence Dogood letter, printed in *The New-England Courant* July 9, 1722. All of the Silence Dogood letters may be found on the Founder's Online section of the National Archives website.

"Silence Dogood, No. 8, 9 July 1722," *Founders Online,* National Archives, founders.archives.gov/documents/ Franklin/01-01-02-0015. [Original source: Leonard W. Labaree, ed., *The Papers of Benjamin Franklin,* vol. 1, *January 6, 1706, through December 31, 1734* (New Haven: Yale University Press, 1959), 27–30.]

Ch. 19: A Tea Party in Boston

1. John Dickinson's thundering condemnation of the Townshend Acts was written in a series of letters, all of them signed merely "A Farmer," which were printed over a period of ten weeks in late 1767 and early 1768 and republished in newspapers all over the colonies. The fragment quoted in this chapter appears in the first letter. All the letters may be found here:

    "Letters From a Farmer in Pennsylvania," Delaware Historical & Cultural Affairs, n.d., history.delaware.gov/john-dickinson-plantation/dickinsonletters/pennsylvania-farmer-letters/.

2. The quotation from Sam Adams was taken from this collection:

    Adams, *Writings*, 336.

3. King George's assertion that the colonists must either submit or triumph is one of the more famous quotations from the history of the War for Independence.

    George III, King of Great Britain, *The Correspondence of King George the Third from 1760 to December 1783*, ed. Sir John Fortescue (London: Frank Cass and Company, 1967), 131, archive.org/details/correspondenceof0003geor/page/130/mode/2up.

Ch. 20: On Lexington Green

1. The complete text of Patrick Henry's fiery speech can be found here:

    "Patrick Henry—Give Me Liberty Or Give Me Death," Avalon Project: Documents in Law, History and Diplomacy, Yale Law School, 2008, avalon.law.yale.edu/18th_century/patrick.asp.

2. George III's comments to Lord North asserting that "blows must decide" were written in a letter dated November 18, 1774. An image of that letter can be seen by visiting the Royal Collection Trust's digital collection:

"Letter from George III to Lord North," Royal Collection Trust, n.d., gpp.rct.uk/GetMultimedia. ashx?db=Catalog&type=default&fname=GEO_MAIN_1917. pdf. [Original source: J. Fortescue, ed., *Correspondence of King George III,* vol. 3, From 1760 to December 1783 (London: Frank Cass and Company, 1927–1928), no. 1556.]

3. Major Pitcairn's letter is quoted in many histories of this period. I found it here:

   Shi, *America,* 132.

4. The phrase "One if by land, and two if by sea" was coined by the American poet Henry W. Longfellow (1807–1882) in his poem "Paul Revere's Ride":

   > *Listen, my children, and you shall hear*
   > *Of the midnight ride of Paul Revere,*
   > *On the eighteenth of April, in Seventy-Five:*
   > *Hardly a man is now alive*
   > *Who remembers that famous day and year.*
   >
   > *He said to his friend, "If the British march*
   > *By land or sea from the town to-night,*
   > *Hang a lantern aloft in the belfry-arch*
   > *Of the North-Church-tower, as a signal-light,—*
   > *One if by land, and two if by sea;*
   > *And I on the opposite shore will be,*
   > *Ready to ride and spread the alarm*
   > *Through every Middlesex village and farm,*
   > *For the country-folk to be up and to arm.*

   Longfellow, "Paul Revere's Ride," st. 1 and 2, "Paul Revere's Ride," Poets.org, Academy of American Poets, poets.org/ poem/paul-reveres-ride.

5. The eyewitness accounts of the events on Lexington Green can be found here:

   Journals of the Continental Congress, Vol. II, May 10– September 20, 1775 (Washington, D.C.: Government

Printing Office, 1905), 28–30, archive.org/details/
journalsofcontin02unit/page/28/mode/2up.

6. Captain John Parker's strong words were quoted by his grandson Theodore.

    Theodore Parker, *Trial of Theodore Parker: For the "Misdemeanor" of a Speech in Faneuil Hall against Kidnapping* (Cambridge, 1855), 22, archive.org/details/
    trialoftheodorep00park/page/220/mode/2up.

7. George Washington's musing upon "the first blood . . . drawn" is found in his diary entry for October 26, 1789:

    "Diary Entry: 26 October 1789, *Founders Online,* National Archives, n.d., founders.archives.gov/documents/
    Washington/01-05-02-0005-0002-0026. [Original source: Donald Jackson and Dorothy Twohig, eds., *The Diaries of George Washington,* vol. 5, *1 July 1786–31 December 1789* (Charlottesville: University Press of Virginia, 1979), 477.]

Ch. 21: The Spirit of 1776

1. The famous command to avoid firing "until you see the white of their eyes" is not original to the Battle of Bunker Hill. It had been urged by various military commanders throughout history. But eyewitness accounts claim that it was certainly shouted that day by Prescott and others.

    Frothingham, Jr., *Siege of Boston,* 140.

2. The comment regarding the dead lying "as thick as sheep in a fold" was made by American Colonel John Stark and is quoted in many sources. I found it here:

    Christian Di Spigna, *Founding Martyr: The Life and Death of Joseph Warren, the American Revolution's Lost Hero* (New York: Crown Publishers, 2018), 182.

3. General Clinton's lament about the high cost of the British victory at Bunker Hill can be found here:

Sir Henry Clinton, *The American Rebellion: Sir Henry Clinton's Narrative of His Campaigns, 1775–1782,* ed. William B. Willcox (New Haven, CT: Yale University Press, 1954), 19.

4. John Adams's comments regarding George Washington's leadership, and Washington's response, can both be found in the National Archives Founders Online, here:

   "Address to the Continental Congress, 16 June 1775," *Founders Online,* National Archives, n.d., founders.archives. gov/documents/Washington/03-01-02-0001. [Original source: Philander D. Chase, ed., *The Papers of George Washington,* Revolutionary War Series, vol. 1, *16 June 1775–15 September 1775* (Charlottesville: University Press of Virginia, 1985), 1–3.]

5. The quotation from Thomas Paine's *Common Sense* can be found in his introduction:

   Paine, *Common Sense,* ___, www.loc.gov/item/30020919/

6. Richard Henry Lee's resolution can be read in full here:

   "Lee Resolution (1776)," National Archives, 2022, www. archives.gov/milestone-documents/lee-resolution. [Original source: Adoption of the Resolution Calling for Independence from England; 7/2/1776; Reports on Administrative Affairs of the Congress; Papers of the Continental Congress, 1774–1789; Records of the Continental and Confederation Congresses and the Constitutional Convention, Record Group 360; National Archives Building, Washington, D.C.]

7. Thomas Jefferson's musing upon the question of independence is quoted by Robert Remini in his *Short History of the United States,* page 40.

   Remini, *Short History,* 40.

Ch. 22: Through the Valley of the Shadow

1. Thomas Paine's quotation regarding the "times that try men's souls" is one of his most famous. It was published

anonymously in an essay entitled "The American Crisis" published in the *Pennsylvania Journal* on December 19, 1776.

"The American Crisis (No. 1) by the author of *Common Sense,*" Library of Congress, n.d., www.loc.gov/resource/rbpe.03902300/?st=text.

2. The British officer's words can be found quoted here:

    Victor Brooks and Robert Hohwald, *How America Fought Its Wars: Military Strategy from the American Revolution to the Civil War* (Conshohocken, PA: Combined Publishing, 1999), 78, archive.org/details/howamericafought0000broo/page/78/mode/2up.

3. "The Valley of the Shadow" is a reference to Psalm 23:4 (KJV): "Yea, though I walk through the valley of the shadow of death, I will fear no evil: for thou art with me; thy rod and thy staff they comfort me."

4. The quotation celebrating Washington's "great and good" victory can be found in many sources. For example:

    Montgomery, *Leading Facts,* 169.

5. Lord North's reaction to the news of the war's end was reported by an eyewitness, Lord Nathaniel Wraxall:

    "Memoirs of Sir Nathaniel Wraxall," Teaching American History, 2022, teachingamericanhistory.org/document/memoirs-of-sir-nathaniel-wraxall/.

Ch. 23: We the People

1. Alexander Hamilton's suggestion that the states devise a new constitution was recorded in a resolution made in September 1876 by the Annapolis Convention, a forerunner to the Constitutional Convention in Philadelphia. The entire resolution can be read here:

    "Annapolis Convention Resolution," Teaching American History, 2022, teachingamericanhistory.org/document/annapolis-convention-resolution/.

2. George Washington's comparison of the Articles of Confederation to a "rope of sand" was made in a letter to Henry Knox on February 28, 1785. The letter can be read in full here:

"From George Washington to Henry Knox, 28 February 1785," *Founders Online*, National Archives, n.d., founders. archives.gov/documents/Washington/04-02-02-0267. [Original source: W. W. Abbot, ed., *The Papers of George Washington,* Confederation Series, vol. 2, *18 July 1784–18 May 1785* (Charlottesville: University Press of Virginia, 1992), 398–401.]

3. Benjamin Franklin's comment that nothing in the world is certain but death and taxes is one of his most oft-cited sayings. It was written in a letter to French scientist Jean-Baptiste LeRoy on November 13, 1789, which can be found here:

Albert Henry Smyth, *The Writings of Benjamin Franklin* (New York: The Macmillan Co., 1907), 68 and 69, archive.org/ details/writingsofbenjam10franuoft/page/68/mode/2up.

Ch. 24: Walking the Wilderness Road

1. Dan's father's comment regarding Dan's shooting is quoted here:

Faragher, *Boone,* 16.

2. Daniel's remarks revealing his determination to walk into the wilderness are taken from his writings and quoted here:

Morgan, *Boone,* 98, 339, and 395.

Ch. 25: The Way Forward

1. Washington's statement that he had been summoned by his country was made in the introductory paragraph of his First Inaugural Address. It can be read in full in the Founders Online archive, here:

"First Inaugural Address: Final Version, 30 April 1789," *Founders Online*, National Archives, n.d., founders.archives.

gov/documents/Washington/05-02-02-0130-0003. [Original source: Dorothy Twohig, ed., *The Papers of George Washington,* Presidential Series, vol. 2, *1 April 1789–15 June 1789* (Charlottesville: University Press of Virginia, 1987), 173–177.]

2. Washington's dying words were recorded by his secretary, Tobias Lear. An account of this can be found here:

    II, 14 December 1799, The Diary Account," *Founders Online,* National Archives, n.d., founders.archives.gov/documents/ Washington/06-04-02-0406-0002. [Original source: The Papers of George Washington, Retirement Series, vol. 4, 20 April 1799–13 December 1799, ed. W. W. Abbot (Charlottesville: University Press of Virginia, 1999), 547–555.]

3. The famous description of George Washington as "first in war, first in peace" comes from a funeral oration written by General Henry "Light-Horse Harry" Lee. This oration can be read in full here:

    "Washington's Funeral Oration," Portraits in Revolution, n.d., www.americanrevolution.com/documents/washington_ funeral_oration_by_henry_lee.

4. John Adams's blessing on the White House is carved into a mantel in the state dining room:

    "Adams's blessing was carved into the state dining room mantel in 1945," White House Historical Association, n.d., www. whitehousehistory.org/photos/adamss-blessing-was-carved-into-the-state-dining-room-mantel-in-1945.

Ch. 26: Way Out West

1. President Jefferson's instructions to Meriwether Lewis can be read in full here:

    "Thomas Jefferson's Instructions to Meriwether Lewis (June 20, 1803)," Encyclopedia Virginia, 2020, encyclopediavirginia. org/entries/thomas-jeffersons-instructions-to-meriwether-lewis-june-20-1803/.

2. The report of Lewis's departure was written by Captain Amos Stoddard to Secretary of War Henry Dearborn on June 3, 1804. It can be found quoted here:

Ambrose, *Undaunted Courage*, 139.

3. The quotation from Meriwether Lewis's journals can be found online here: "May 26, 1805 [Lewis]," Journals of the Lewis & Clark Expedition, n.d., lewisandclarkjournals.unl.edu/item/lc.jrn.1805-05-26.

Ch. 27: Over the Pathless Oceans

1. The eulogy for Nathaniel Bowditch is discussed here:

"Nathaniel Bowditch," Boston Athenaeum, 2014, web.archive.org/web/20220928194020/https://www.bostonathenaeum.org/library/book-recommendations/athenaeum-authors/nathaniel-bowditch.

Ch. 28: "Don't Give Up the Ship": The War of 1812

1. Oliver Hazard Perry's remark regarding the Battle of Lake Erie as "the most important day of my life" was made to one of the ship's crewmen, Purser Hambleton. The incident is described here:

Skaggs, *Oliver Hazard Perry*, 107.

2. Perry's message to William Henry Harrison is one of the most famous quotations from the War of 1812 and can be found recorded in many sources. In the above book, you can find it on p. 118. The entire note reads as follows:

Dear General,

We have met the enemy and they are ours. Two Ships, two Brigs, one Schooner, and one Sloop.

Yours, with very great respect and esteem,

O. H. Perry

Skaggs, *Oliver Hazard Perry*, 118.

Ch. 29: By The Dawn's Early Light

1. The order to "destroy and lay waste" was sent on July 18, 1814, by Vice Admiral Sir Alexander Cochrane to Rear Admiral George Cockburn who was in command of the English troops. The order read as follows:

   "You are hereby required and directed to destroy and lay waste such towns and districts as you may find assailable. . . . you will spare merely the lives of the unarmed American inhabitants of the United States."

   Ernest Cruickshank, ed., *The Documentary History of the Campaign on the Niagara Frontier in 1814*, 2 vols. (Welland, 1896), 414 and 415, archive.org/details/documentaryhisto12lund_0/page/414/mode/2up.

2. The huge flag at Fort McHenry—large enough that "the British will have no difficulty seeing it from a distance"—is discussed in numerous histories of the War of 1812. The National Park Service tells the story in its website for the Fort McHenry National Monument:

   "The Great Garrison Flag," National Park Service, U.S. Department of the Interior, September 8, 2020, www.nps.gov/fomc/learn/historyculture/the-great-garrison-flag.htm

3. Francis Scott Key's original manuscript of "The Star-Spangled Banner" can be viewed here:

   "Key, Francis Scott. Original Manuscript of 'Star Spangled Banner,'" Library of Congress, n.d., www.loc.gov/item/2016865604/.

Selected Bibliography

Adams, Samuel. *The Writings of Samuel Adams,* Vol. II. Edited by Harry Alonzo Cushing. New York: G.P. Putnam's Sons, 1906.

Ambrose, Stephen E. *Undaunted Courage: Meriwether Lewis, Thomas Jefferson, and the Opening of the American West.* New York: Simon & Schuster, 2013.

Borneman, Walter R. *The French and Indian War: Deciding the Fate of North America.* New York: Harper Perennial, 2007.

Bradford, William. *Of Plymouth Plantation, 1620–1647.* Edited by Samuel Eliot Morison. New York: Alfred A. Knopf, 1952.

Chernow, Ron. *Washington: A Life.* New York: Penguin Books, 2011.

Columbus, Christopher. *The Journal of Christopher Columbus (during His First Voyage, 1492–93), and Documents Relating the Voyages of John Cabot and Gaspar Corte Real.* Translated by Clements R. Markham. London: Hakluyt Society, 1893.

de Blij, H. J., ed. *Atlas of North America.* New York: Oxford University Press, 2005.

Dolin, Eric Jay. *Black Flags, Blue Waters: The Epic History of America's Most Notorious Pirates.* New York: Liveright Publishing Corporation, a division of W.W. Norton & Company, 2019.

Donehoo, George Patterson. *Pennsylvania, a History.* New York: Lewis Historical Pub. Corp., 1931.

"Early Americas Digital Archive (EADA)," University of Maryland Libraries, n.d., eada.lib.umd.edu/.

Faragher, John Mack. *Daniel Boone: The Life and Legend of an American Pioneer.* Norwalk: The Easton Press, 1993.

"Founders Online," The U.S. National Archives and Records Administration, 2010, founders.archives.gov.

Frothingham, Jr., Richard. *History of the Siege of Boston, and of the Battles of Lexington, Concord, and Bunker Hill.* Boston: Charles C. Little and James Brown, 1851. www.google.com/books/edition/_/ p8rTAAAAMAAJ?hl=en&gbpv=1.

Gocher, W. H. *Wadsworth, or the Charter Oak.* Hartford, CT: W.H. Gocher, 1904.

Goetzmann, William H., and Glyndwr Williams. *The Atlas of North American Exploration: From the Norse Voyages to the Race to the Pole.* Norman: University Of Oklahoma Press, 1998.

Hayes, Derek. *America Discovered: A Historical Atlas of North American Exploration.* Vancouver: Douglas & McIntyre, 2009.

Hickey, Donald R. *The War of 1812: A Short History.* Urbana: University of Illinois Press, 2012.

Isaacson, Walter. *Benjamin Franklin: An American Life.* New York: Thorndike Press, 2003.

Jefferson, Thomas. *Notes on the State of Virginia.* London: John Stockdale, 1787. archive.org/details/notesonstateofvi1787jeff/ page/12/mode/2up.

"Journals of the Continental Congress: Continental Congress and the Constitutional Convention," The Library of Congress: American Memory, n.d., memory.loc.gov/ammem/amlaw/ lwjc.html?loclr=blogadm.

Lepore, Jill. *These Truths: A History of the United States.* New York: W. W. Norton & Company, 2019.

Marrin, Albert. *The War for Independence: The Story of the American Revolution.* New York: Atheneum, 1988.

Middleton, Richard, and Anne S. Lombard. *Colonial America: A History to 1763.* Malden, MA: Wiley-Blackwell, 2011.

Montgomery, D H. *The Leading Facts of American History.* Boston: Ginn And Company, 1920.

Morgan, Robert. *Boone: A Biography*. Chapel Hill, NC: Algonquin Books of Chapel Hill, 2007.

Morison, Samuel Eliot. *The Oxford History of the American People*. New York: Oxford University Press, 1965.

Myers, Lorraine B., Richard Carlson, and John S. Bowman, eds.. *Illustrated Atlas of Native American History*. Edison, NJ: Chartwell Books, 1999.

Paine, Thomas. *Common Sense: The Rights of Man and Other Essential Writings of Thomas Paine*. Lexington, KY: Empire Books, 2013.

Philbrick, Nathaniel. *Mayflower: Voyage, Community, War*. New York: Penguin Books, 2007.

Remini, Robert Vincent. *A Short History of the United States*. New York: HarperCollins Publishers, 2008.

Santacroce, Joe. "The Four Voyages of Henry Hudson." *The Newburgh History Blog*, February 19, 2019, newburghhistoryblog.com/the-four-voyages-of-henry-hudson-by-joe-santacroce/.

Shi, David Emory. *America: A Narrative History*. New York: W. W. Norton & Company, 2019.

Skaggs, David Curtis. *Oliver Hazard Perry: Honor, Courage, and Patriotism in the Early U.S. Navy*. Annapolis, MD: Naval Institute Press, 2006.

Taylor, Alan. *American Colonies: The Settling of North America*. Edited by Eric Foner. New York: Penguin Books, 2001.

Thompson, C. Bradley. *America's Revolutionary Mind: A Moral History of the American Revolution and the Declaration That Defined It*. New York: Encounter Books, 2019.

Townsend, Kenneth William, and Mark A. Nicholas. *First Americans: A History of Native Peoples*. Combined Volume. New York: Routledge Taylor & Francis Group, 2016.

"US Maps," GIS Geography, 2022, gisgeography.com/category/us-maps/.

Vespucci, Amerigo. *The Letters of Amerigo Vespucci and Other Documents Illustrative of His Career*. Translated by Clements R. Markham. London: The Hakluyt Society, 1894.

Weinstein, Allen, and David Rubel. *The Story of America: Freedom and Crisis from Settlement to Superpower*. New York: Dorling Kindersley, 2002.

Wilbur, C. Keith. *Early Explorers of North America*. Philadelphia: Chelsea House Publishers, 1997.

Wood, Gordon S. *The Creation of the American Republic: 1776-1787*. Chapel Hill: The University of North Carolina Press, 1998.

Image Sources

Chapter 1: An American Day
"*The geography of the contiguous United States*": Map of the contiguous United States, The National Map, National Geospatial Program. Map services and data available from U.S. Geological Survey, National Geospatial Program. Accessed March 1, 2023. www.usgs.gov/programs/national-geospatial-program/national-map.

Chapter 2: Until 1941
"*A kiva in present-day Utah*": Historic American Buildings Survey, National Park Service, Donald W. Dickensheets, photographer, *Kiva (Large), Bland, Sandoval County, NM,* June 1940, photograph, Library of Congress, Prints and Photographs Division, www.loc.gov/resource/hhh.nm0008. photos/?sp=1.

"*Pueblo cliff homes at Chaco Canyon, New Mexico*": National Park Service, *View of Cliff Palace from Above,* date unknown, photograph, NPS website photo gallery: Cliff Dwellings of Mesa Verde National Park, www.nps.gov/media/photo/gallery.htm?pg=1978152&id=FF496A0D-155D-451F-6780618AC2528471. NPS photo.

"*The Serpent Mound in present-day Ohio*": *Serpent Mound photograph,* ca. 1960-1980, photograph, Ohio History Connection Selections, ohiomemory.org/digital/collection/p267401coll32/id/14887. Courtesy of the Ohio History Connection.

"*The Bighorn Medicine Wheel in present-day Wyoming*": U.S. Forest Service, Medicine Wheel, date unknown, photograph, Wikimedia Commons website, commons.wikimedia.org/wiki/File:MedicineWheel.jpg.

Chapter 4: Searching for Cipango

"*Christopher Columbus*": Johann Theodor de Bry, *Christopher Columbus*, 1595, engraving, Library of Congress, Prints and Photographs Division, www.loc.gov/resource/cph.3a39649/.

"*Columbus's Voyages*": H. C. Robertson, *Columbus' Voyages*, 1898, 88 x 64 cm, in *Robertson's Geographic-historical Series Illustrating the History of America and the United States from 1492 to [1898]* (Chicago: R.O. Evans and Co., 1898), 4, Library of Congress, Geography and Map Division, www.loc.gov/resource/g3701sm.gct00077/?sp=4&st=image&r=0.163,0.347,0.632,0.345,0.

Chapter 5: The Fourth Part of the World

"*Map of the New World created by Martin Waldseemüller in 1507*": Martin Waldseemüller, cartographer, *Universalis cosmographia secundum Ptholomaei traditionem et Americi Vespucii alioru[m]que lustrationes* (the Waldseemuller map), 1507, 1 map on 12 sheets ; 128 x 233 cm., sheets 46 x 63 cm. or smaller, Library of Congress, Geography and Map Division, www.loc.gov/resource/g3200.ct000725.

Chapter 8: The Lost Colony

"*Sir Walter Raleigh*": Simon van de Passe (1591-1644), *Sir Walter Raleigh: The true and lively portraiture of the honourable and learned Knight S. Walter Raleigh*, date unknown, engraving, Library of Congress, Prints and Photographs Division, www.loc.gov/resource/cph.3a06535/.

"*Queen Elizabeth I of England*": W. Faithorne, Portraits: *Queen Elizabeth, Lord Burleigh and Sir Walsingham*, date unknown, medium unknown, Wellcome Collection, wellcomecollection.org/works/braw3ytw. License: Attribution 4.0 International (CC BY 4.0): creativecommons.org/licenses/by/4.0/legalcode. Credit: Portraits: Queen Elizabeth, Lord Burleigh and Sir Walsingham. Wellcome Collection.

Chapter 9: Work to Eat

"*One of the original buildings of the settlement at Jamestown*": National Parks Gallery, *Views of Jamestown National Historic*

Site, Colonial National Historical Park, Virginia, 1980–1999, photograph, PICRYL website, picryl.com/media/views-of-jamestown-national-historic-site-colonial-national-historical-park-376f44.

"Chesapeake Bay": United States Coast Survey, cartographer, *Chesapeake Bay,* 1862, 36 x 43 cm, Library of Congress, Geography and Map Division, www.loc.gov/resource/g3842c.ct008682/.

"Statue of Pocahontas at Historic Jamestown": Carol M. Highsmith, *Pocahontas statue at Historic Jamestowne,* November 2019, photograph, Library of Congress, Prints and Photographs Division, www.loc.gov/resource/highsm.61497/.

"Page from Captain John Smith's book": Captain John Smith, title page to *A True Relation of Such Occurrences and Accidents of Noate as Hath Happened in Virginia* (London, 1608), National Park Service website, www.nps.gov/articles/000/john-smith-writings.htm.

Chapter 10: Across the Vast and Furious Ocean
"The Mayflower Compact": William Bradford, *Page from Bradford's History, on which is the Mayflower Compact,* date unknown, photograph, transcribed in William Bradford, *Of Plymouth Plantation: 1620–1647* (New York: Random House, 1981), 83, PICRYL website, picryl.com/media/page-from-bradfords-history-on-which-is-the-mayflower-compact-cb46f7.

Chapter 12: The Gifts of Charles II
"Early map of the Virginia colony": Richard Blome, cartographer, *Map of Virginia, North Carolina, and South Carolina,* 1709, NYPL Lionel Pincus and Princess Firyal Map Division, PICRYL website, picryl.com/media/map-of-virginia-north-carolina-and-south-carolina-a12237.

Chapter 13: Noble Experiments
"William Penn's 'Frame of Government'": William Penn, title page to *The Frame of the Government of the Province of Pennsylvania* (pub. city unknown, 1682), British Library

website, www.bl.uk/collection-items/the-frame-of-the-government-of-the-province-of-pennsilvania.

Chapter 14: The Charter Oak
"The Virginia House of Burgesses in Williamsburg, Virginia": Frances Benjamin Johnston, *House of Burgesses in the Capitol, Williamsburg, James City County, Virginia,* ca. 1930–1939, photograph, Carnegie Survey of the Architecture of the South, Library of Congress, Prints and Photographs Division, www.loc.gov/resource/csas.05799/.

Chapter 17: Farewell, Acadia
"Benjamin Franklin's 'Join, or Die' cartoon": Benjamin Franklin, *Join, or Die,* May 1754, print of woodcut, Library of Congress, www.loc.gov/resource/cph.3g05315/.

Chapter 18: Poor Richard
"Poor Richard's Almanack": Benjamin Franklin, title page to *Poor Richard's Almanack* (Philadelphia, 1748), Library of Congress, Prints and Photographs Division, www.loc.gov/resource/cph.3b22676/.

Chapter 20: On Lexington Green
"Monument at Lexington Green, Massachusetts": Detroit Publishing Company, *Line of the Minutemen memorial on the Green, Lexington, Mass.,* 1900–1915, photograph, Library of Congress, Prints and Photographs Division, www.loc.gov/resource/det.4a27600/.

Chapter 21: The Spirit of 1776
"Thomas Paine's Common Sense": Thomas Paine, title page to *Common Sense* (Philadelphia, 1776), Library of Congress, Rare Book and Special Collections Division, www.loc.gov/resource/cph.3a13073/.

"The Declaration of Independence": Thomas Jefferson, *Engrossed Declaration of Independence* (August 1776), The Library of Congress, www.loc.gov/resource/gdcwdl.wdl_02705/?sp=1&r=-0.378,-0.055,1.734,0.938,0. Credit: World Digital Library.

Chapter 22: Through the Valley of the Shadow

"*Fort Ticonderoga*": Mwanner [pseud.], *Fort Ticonderoga, Ticonderoga, New York,* May 2009, photograph, Wikimedia Commons website, commons.wikimedia.org/wiki/ File:Fort_Ticonderoga,_Ticonderoga,_NY.jpg. License: creativecommons.org/licenses/by-sa/3.0/legalcode.

"*George Washington*": Augustus Weidenbach, artist, after Gilbert Stuart, artist, *George Washington,* 1876, chromolithograph on paper, Library of Congress, Prints and Photographs Division, www.loc.gov/resource/pga.01368/.

Chapter 23: We the People

"*The Pennsylvania State House, now called Independence Hall*": Carol M. Highsmith, *Independence Hall at Independence National Historical Park in Philadelphia, Pennsylvania,* July 2013, photograph, Library of Congress, Prints & Photographs Division, www.loc.gov/resource/highsm.56734/. Reproduction number LC-DIG-highsm-56734.

"*The Constitution of the United States*": United States Constitutional Convention, *Constitution of the United States* (September 1787), Library of Congress, www.archives.gov/ founding-docs/constitution. Credit: World Digital Library. Original resource at: U.S. National Archives and Records Administration.

Chapter 24: Walking the Wilderness Road

"*Early map of the Kentucky territory, originally part of Virginia*": John Filson, cartographer, and Henry D. Pursell, engraver, *This map of Kentucke, drawn from actual observations is inscribed with the most perfect respect to the honorable the Congress of the United States of America, and to his excellcy. George Washington, late commander in chief of their army,* 1784, 1:633,600; 10 miles to an in. scale, 51 x 46 cm. fold. to 26 x 17 cm., Library of Congress, Geography and Map Division, www.loc.gov/ resource/g3950.ct010413/.

"*Daniel Boone*": Unknown engraver, after painting by Alonzo Chappel, *Daniel Boone,* circa 1861, engraving, in Evert A.

Duyckinck, *National Portrait Gallery of Eminent Americans. . . From Original Full Length Paintings by Alonzo Chappel* (New York: Johnson, Fry, & Company, 1862), vol. 1, behind 183, play.google.com/books/reader?id=TypTAAAcAAJ&pg=GBS. PA182-IA2&hl=en, Wikimedia Commons website, commons. wikimedia.org/wiki/File:Boone_by_Chappel.jpg.

Chapter 25: The Way Forward
"(left to right) Presidents George Washington, John Adams, and Thomas Jefferson":

Gilbert Stuart, *George Washington,* 1821, oil on wood, 26 3/8 x 21 5/8 in., National Gallery of Art, www.nga.gov/collection/art-object-page.56916.html. Courtesy National Gallery of Art, Washington.

Gilbert Stuart, *John Adams,* 1821, oil on wood, 26 x 21 7/16 in., National Gallery of Art, www.nga.gov/collection/art-object-page.56913.html. Courtesy National Gallery of Art, Washington.

Gilbert Stuart, *Thomas Jefferson,* 1821, oil on wood, 26 x 21 7/16 in., National Gallery of Art, www.nga.gov/collection/art-object-page.69391.html. Courtesy National Gallery of Art, Washington.

Chapter 26: Way Out West
"Page from the journals of the Corps of Discovery": William Clark, page from *Clark Family Collection: Volume 2. [for] his Journal No. 2, Page 73,* William Clark's drawing and description of a grouse, March 1806, Missouri Historical Society Online Collections, mohistory.org/collections/item/ N26589.

"The Louisiana Purchase": Department of the Interior, General Land Office, *Map of the Louisiana Purchase Territory,* 1903, National Archives Catalog, catalog.archives.gov/id/594889.

Chapter 27: Over the Pathless Oceans
"The New American Practical Navigator by Nathaniel Bowditch": Nathaniel Bowditch, title page to *The New*

American Practical Navigator (Newburyport, MA, 1802), Smithsonian Libraries, library.si.edu/digital-library/book/newamericanpract00bowd. Courtesy of the Smithsonian Libraries and Archives.

"Statue of Nathaniel Bowditch in Salem, Massachusetts": Daderot [pseud.], Mount Auburn Cemetery—*Nathaniel Bowditch Memorial by Robert Ball Hughes,* May 2008, photograph, Wikimedia Commons website, commons. wikimedia.org/wiki/File:Mount_Auburn_Cemetery_-_ Nathaniel_Bowditch_memorial_by_Robert_Ball_Hughes.jpg.

Chapter 29: By the Dawn's Early Light
"Routes of the principal explorers of the United States": Frank Bond, cartographer, *Map of the United States Showing Routes of the Principal Explorers from 1501 to 1844,* 1907, 19 x 29 cm, Library of Congress, Geography and Map Division, www.loc. gov/resource/g3701s.np000053/?r=0.004,0.497,0.36,0.195,0.

Made in the USA
Coppell, TX
27 June 2024

33997553R00138